FAITH
FITNESS

AND
FOOD
for Women

DaySpring

LIVE YOUR FAITH

Bible verses were taken from the following translations:

KJV: The Holy Bible, King James Version

HCSB: Scripture quotations marked HCSB®, are taken from the Holman Christian Standard Bible®, Copyright © 1999, 2000, 2002, 2003, 2009 by Holman Bible Publishers. Used by permission. HCSB® is a federally registered trademark of Holman Bible Publishers.

Scriptures marked MSG are taken from the THE MESSAGE: THE BIBLE IN CONTEMPORARY ENGLISH (MSG), copyright©1993, 1994, 1995, 1996, 2000, 2001, 2002. Used by permission of NavPress Publishing Group.

NASB: Scripture quotations taken from the New American Standard Bible®, Copyright © 1960, 1962, 1963, 1968, 1971, 1972, 1973, 1975, 1977, 1995 by The Lockman Foundation Used by permission.

NCV: Scripture taken from the New Century Version. Copyright © 1987, 1988, 1991 by Thomas Nelson, Inc. Used by permission. All rights reserved.

NIV: Scripture quotations marked (NIV) are taken from the Holy Bible, New International Version®, NIV®. Copyright © 1973, 1978, 1984, 2011 by Biblica, Inc.™ Used by permission of Zondervan. All rights reserved worldwide. www.zondervan. com The "NIV" and "New International Version" are trademarks registered in the United States Patent and Trademark Office by Biblica, Inc.™

NKJV: Scripture taken from the New King James Version. Copyright © 1982 by Thomas Nelson, Inc. Used by permission. All rights reserved.

NLT: Holy Bible, New Living Translation, copyright © 1996, 2004, 2007 by Tyndale House Foundation. Used by permission of Tyndale House Publishers, Inc. All rights reserved.

Cover design by Kim Russell | Wahoo Designs

ISBN: 9781684089871

CONTENTS

INTRODUCTION

Faith, fitness, and food: three very important words. But the greatest of these is faith. So this book focuses, first and foremost, on the need to honor God and walk in the footsteps of His only begotten Son. But this text also addresses the other two topics in its title: food and fitness. So, if you're serious about establishing healthier habits and achieving personal goals related to weight and fitness, you've come to the right place.

The Bible is the ultimate guidebook for Christian readers—like you—who seek God's wisdom and His truth. The ideas on these pages are intended to remind you that God's Word is the final word when it comes to matters of spiritual health and your physical well-being.

Health is a gift from the Creator. What you do with that gift is determined, to a surprising extent, by you. If you squander your health—or if you take it for granted—you do a profound disservice to yourself and to the people who care about you. But God has other plans. He instructs you to treat your body like a temple: with appropriate reverence and utmost care.

The health tips in this text are no substitute for a one-on-one consultation with your personal physician. But if you seek to enhance your spiritual, emotional, and physical health, the ideas on these pages will help. Yet they offer no shortcuts. Healthy living is a journey, not a destination, and that journey requires discipline. If you're willing to make the daily pilgrimage toward improved health, rest assured that God is taking careful note of your progress. And you can rest assured that He's quietly urging you to take the next step.

1

FAITH, FITNESS, AND FOOD

For truly I say to you, if you have faith as a mustard seed, you shall say to this mountain, "Move from here to there" and it shall move; and nothing shall be impossible to you.

MATTHEW 17:20 NASB

Countless books have been written on the topics of health, fitness, and diet. But if you're a Christian, you probably already own at least *one* copy—perhaps *several* copies—of the world's foremost guide to spiritual, physical, and emotional health. That book is the Holy Bible. And while this book addresses all three topics contained in its title, it will focus on the most important word in its title. That word is *faith*.

The Bible makes it clear: faith is powerful. With it, you can move mountains. With faith, you can achieve goals that might otherwise seem far beyond your reach. Strengthened by your faith, you can rise above the challenges of everyday life and live victoriously, whatever your circumstances.

Are you prepared to begin moving those personal mountains in your own life? If so, God is ready to help. But if your spiritual batteries are in need of recharging, don't be discouraged. The Father's strength is always available to those who seek it.

As you consider ways to enhance your physical, emotional, and spiritual fitness, remember that God is your greatest resource. Take everything to Him in prayer. When you do, you'll soon discover that you and your Creator, working together, can indeed move mountains. So with no further delay, let the mountain-moving begin.

More FROM GOD'S WORD

Don't be afraid, because I am your God.
I will make you strong and will help you;
I will support you with my right hand that saves you.

ISAIAH 41:10 NCV

Blessed are they that have not seen,
and yet have believed.

JOHN 20:29 KJV

All things are possible for the one who believes.

MARK 9:23 NCV

And he said unto her, Daughter,
thy faith hath made thee whole;
go in peace, and be whole . . .

MARK 5:34 KJV

Don't be afraid. Only believe.

MARK 5:36 HCSB

ABOUT FAITH

*Shout the shout of faith. Nothing can withstand
the triumphant faith that links itself to omnipotence.
The secret of all successful living lies in this shout of faith.*

HANNAH WHITALL SMITH

*I have learned that faith means trusting in advance
what will only make sense in reverse.*

PHILIP YANCEY

*Faith points us beyond our problems
to the hope we have in Christ.*

BILLY GRAHAM

*Faith is not merely holding on to God.
It is God holding on to you.*

CORRIE TEN BOOM

*Faith does not concern itself with the entire journey.
One step is enough.*

LETTIE COWMAN

Food Tip

Know Your Calorie Budget

Look up your suggested daily calorie intake (it's online) based on your gender, age, and level of physical activity. When you know your calorie budget, you can plan your meals accordingly.

Fitness Tip

See Your Doctor

If you're about to begin a new physical fitness regimen, consult your physician *before* you make dramatic changes in your exercise program *or* your diet.

Today's Focus

Remember that you and God,
working together, can move mountains.

2

THE TIME IS NOW

But prove yourselves doers of the word,
and not merely hearers who delude themselves.

JAMES 1:22 NASB

Proper diet and physical fitness, like all the other aspects of your life, begin and end with God. If you'd like to adopt a healthier lifestyle, God is willing to help. In fact, if you sincerely wish to create a healthier you—either physically, emotionally, or spiritually—God is anxious to be your silent partner in that endeavor. But if you're unwilling to begin, if you're determined to keep putting off until tomorrow what needs to be done today, God is perfectly willing to wait.

When an important challenge needs to be tackled, the best time to tackle it is now, not later. But we're tempted to do otherwise. When the task at hand is hard, we're tempted to procrastinate. But procrastination is the enemy of progress and a stumbling block on the path to success.

So, if you'd like to improve your diet, or if you'd like to increase your physical stamina, ask God to give you the strength, the wisdom, and the determination to get started today. And while you're at it, use this time-tested formula for success: pray as if everything depended on the Lord and work as if everything depended on you. When you do, you'll be amazed at the blessings that the Father bestows upon those who ask for His help . . . and then get busy doing their fair share of the work.

More FROM GOD'S WORD

For the kingdom of God is not a matter of talk but of power.

I CORINTHIANS 4:20 HCSB

Therefore, whenever we have the opportunity,
we should do good to everyone,
especially to those in the family of faith.

GALATIANS 6:10 NLT

When you make a vow to God, do not delay to fulfill it.
He has no pleasure in fools; fulfill your vow.

ECCLESIASTES 5:4 NIV

Well done, good and faithful servant;
you were faithful over a few things,
I will make you ruler over many things.
Enter into the joy of your lord.

MATTHEW 25:21 NKJV

Therefore, with your minds ready for action,
be serious and set your hope completely on the grace
to be brought to you at the revelation of Jesus Christ.

I PETER 1:13 HCSB

About Doing It Now, Not Later

Many people are in a rut and a rut is nothing but a grave—
with both ends kicked out.

Vance Havner

Authentic faith cannot help but act.

Beth Moore

There's some task which the God of all the universe,
the great Creator, has for you to do,
and which will remain undone and incomplete until,
by faith and obedience, you step into the will of God.

Alan Redpath

What is needed for happy effectual service
is simply to put your work into the Lord's hand,
and leave it there.

Hannah Whitall Smith

The one word in the spiritual vocabulary is now.

Oswald Chambers

FOOD TIP

Keep a Food Journal

If you're overweight, you should strongly consider keeping
a written record of all the foods and drinks you consume
during the day. Studies have demonstrated that keeping
an accurate food journal can help curb overeating.

FITNESS TIP

It's Part of God's Plan for You

Physical, emotional, and spiritual fitness are all part of God's
plan for you. But it's up to you to make certain that a
healthy lifestyle is a fundamental part of your plan too.

TODAY'S FOCUS

Look for things that you've been putting off. Then ask God to
help you accomplish the important things that you've left undone.

3

DON'T GO ON A DIET!

*Do you like honey? Don't eat too much of it,
or it will make you sick!*

PROVERBS 25:16 NLT

If you want to lose weight, please don't go on a diet! Why? The answer, simply put, is that most diets don't work. In fact, one study that examined the results of popular diets conducted that nearly 100 percent of dieters suffered "almost complete relapse after three to five years." In other words, dieters almost always return to their pre-diet weights, or to even higher weight levels. So, if you need to lose weight, forget about fad diets and focus, instead, on changing your lifestyle.

Your current weight is the result of the number of calories that you have consumed during your lifetime versus the number of calories that you've burned. If you want to lose weight, then you must burn more calories (by engaging in more vigorous physical activities), or take in fewer calories (by eating more sensibly), or both. It's as simple as that.

Many of us are remarkably ill-informed and amazingly apathetic about the foods we eat. We feast on high-fat fast foods. We swoon over sweets. We order up—and promptly pack away—prodigious portions. The result is a society in which too many of us become the human equivalents of the portions we purchase: oversized.

A healthier strategy, of course, is to pay more attention to the nutritional properties of our foods and less attention to their taste. But for those of us who have become accustomed to large quantities of full-flavored, high-calorie foods, old memories indeed die hard.

Should we count every calorie that we ingest from now until the day the Good Lord calls us home? Probably not. When we focus too intently upon weight reduction, we may make weight loss even harder to achieve. Instead, we should eliminate from our diets the foods that are obviously bad for us and we should eat more of the foods that are obviously good for us. And of course, we should eat sensible amounts, not prodigious portions.

How hard is it for us to know the nutritional properties of the foods we eat? Not very hard. In the grocery store, almost every food item is clearly marked. In fast-food restaurants, the fat and calorie contents of entrees are posted on the wall.

As informed adults, we have access to all the information we need to make healthy dietary choices. Now it's up to each of us to make wise dietary choices, or not. Those choices are ours, and so, by the way, are their consequences.

Therefore, whether you eat or drink,
or whatever you do, do everything for God's glory.

1 CORINTHIANS 10:31 HCSB

Eating Sensibly

*The key to healthy eating is moderation
and managing what you eat every day.*

JOHN MAXWELL

Eat to live, not live to eat.

BEN FRANKLIN

*The permanent pleasure associated with eating well—
such as better health, higher energy, more restful sleep,
looking your best, improved work performance,
and a happier frame of mind—
usually outweighs the temporary pleasure of the taste.*

DR. BEN LERNER

*You can look at your calorie count in the same way
you might look at a bank account. Every mouthful of food
is a deposit and every activity that requires energy
is a withdrawal. If we deposit more than we withdraw,
our surplus grows larger and larger.*

JOHN MAXWELL

*Food ought to be a refreshment to the body,
and not a burden.*

ST. BONAVENTURE

FOOD TIP
Crash Diets Always Crash

Don't fall for extreme diets. Don't try to starve yourself,
and fall into the yo-yo diet trap. Instead, adopt healthy
habits you can live with for the rest of your life.

FITNESS TIP
Slow Down, Take a Deep Breath, and Talk to God

As you make health-related choices throughout the day,
slow down and ask yourself this question:
Is this how God wants me to take care of my body?

TODAY'S FOCUS

Think about the long-term benefits of eating sensibly.
And think about the long-term costs of poor food choices.

4

GETTING A FRESH START

Do not remember the former things,
nor consider the things of old.
Behold, I will do a new thing.

ISAIAH 43:18–19 NKJV

Perhaps you've decided it's time to get serious about improving your health. If so, you have the perfect Partner to help you get a fresh start—a new way of thinking and a new way of living. Your Heavenly Father has the power to make all things new, including you. When you go to Him with a sincere heart and willing hands, He will renew your spirit and redirect your steps.

Are you searching for a new path? If so, the Lord will most certainly give you a fresh start. He's prepared to help you change your thoughts, rearrange your priorities, modify your diet, improve your fitness, and transform your life. But it doesn't stop there. He's also promised to forgive your sins, to forget your failings, and to protect you throughout all eternity. All you must do is ask.

Today is the perfect day to begin. And it's the perfect day to have a heart-to-heart talk with your Creator. If you're ready to get started, He's ready to help.

More FROM GOD'S WORD

*Your old sinful self has died, and your
new life is kept with Christ in God.*

COLOSSIANS 3:3 NCV

*There is one thing I always do. Forgetting the past
and straining toward what is ahead, I keep trying to reach
the goal and get the prize for which God called me . . .*

PHILIPPIANS 3:13–14 NCV

*Then the One seated on the throne said,
"Look! I am making everything new."*

REVELATION 21:5 HCSB

*"For I know the plans I have for you"—
[this is] the LORD's declaration—"plans for [your] welfare,
not for disaster, to give you a future and a hope."*

JEREMIAH 29:11 HCSB

*You are being renewed in the spirit of your minds;
you put on the new man, the one created according
to God's likeness in righteousness and purity of the truth.*

EPHESIANS 4:23–24 HCSB

About New Beginnings

God specializes in giving people a fresh start.

Rick Warren

What saves a man is to take a step.
Then another step.

C. S. Lewis

Are you in earnest? Seize this very minute.
What you can do, or dream you can, begin it.
Boldness has genius, power, and magic in it.

Johann Wolfgang von Goethe

The best preparation for the future
is the present well seen to, and the last duty done.

George MacDonald

Each day you must say to yourself,
"Today I am going to begin."

Jean Pierre de Caussade

FOOD TIP

The Average Calorie Count Isn't for Everybody

Two thousand calories per day isn't for everyone. You may need more or fewer calories depending on your age and level of activity.

FITNESS TIP

Get Started Today

If you feel the need to improve your physical health, don't wait for New Year's Day; don't even wait until tomorrow. When it comes to the important business of improving your physical health, the time to get started is now. Later may be too late.

TODAY'S FOCUS

Consider the importance of starting
your new fitness regimen now.

5

YOUR REGULAR APPOINTMENT WITH GOD

*Morning by morning he wakens me and opens
my understanding to his will. The Sovereign LORD
has spoken to me, and I have listened . . .*

ISAIAH 50:4–5 NLT

Each day of your life has 1,440 minutes, and God deserves a few of them. And you deserve the experience of spending a few quiet minutes every morning with Him. So, if you haven't already done so, establish the habit of spending time with God every day of the week. It's a habit that will change your day and revolutionize your life. When you give the Lord your undivided attention, everything changes, including you.

Your early-morning devotional is the perfect time to ask for the Lord's help. If you're striving to eat healthier food, or if you're determined to improve your physical fitness, God can give you the strength you need to accomplish those goals. When you ask, He hears. And He will help.

Every new day is a gift from the Creator, a gift that allows each of us to say, "Thank you," by spending time with Him. When we put God first, we are inevitably blessed. No exceptions.

More FROM GOD'S WORD

It is good to give thanks to the LORD,
And to sing praises to Your name, O Most High.

PSALM 92:1 NKJV

Thy word is a lamp unto my feet, and a light unto my path.

PSALM 119:105 KJV

Early the next morning, while it was still dark, Jesus woke
and left the house. He went to a lonely place, where he prayed.

MARK 1:35 NCV

But grow in the grace and knowledge
of our Lord and Savior Jesus Christ.
To Him be the glory both now and to the day of eternity.

II PETER 3:18 HCSB

Heaven and earth will pass away,
but My words will never pass away.

MATTHEW 24:35 HCSB

About Your Daily Devotional

*Let it be your business every day, in the secrecy
of the inner chamber, to meet the holy God.
You will be repaid for the trouble it may cost you.
The reward will be sure and rich.*

Andrew Murray

*Whatever is your best time in the day,
give that to communion with God.*

Hudson Taylor

Doesn't God deserve the best minutes of your day?

Billy Graham

Begin each day with God. It will change your priorities.

Elizabeth George

*Relying on God has to begin all over again
every day as if nothing had yet been done.*

C. S. Lewis

FOOD TIP

What's the Serving Size on the Label?

Pay close attention to the serving size when comparing food labels. Low calories per serving don't do you much good if the serving size is so small you're bound to eat two or three!

FITNESS TIP

Ask for Help Every Day

As you spend time with God each morning, ask Him for the strength and the wisdom to treat your body with the respect it deserves. If you ask, and keep asking, He will answer.

TODAY'S FOCUS

Think about the importance of spending time with God every day.

6

Establishing the Right Habits

And so, dear brothers and sisters, I plead with you to give your bodies to God. Let them be a living and holy sacrifice— the kind he will find acceptable.

ROMANS 12:1 NLT

It's an old adage, perhaps trite, but most certainly true: First, you make your habits, and then your habits make you. Some habits are character-builders: they inevitably bring you closer to the path God intends for your life. Other habits lead you away from His path. If you sincerely desire to improve your physical, spiritual, or emotional health, you must honestly examine the habits that knit together to form the fabric of your day. And you must abandon the habits that are self-destructive, self-defeating, or displeasing to God.

Perhaps you've tried to become a more disciplined person, but you're still falling back into old patterns. If so, don't get discouraged; just keep praying.

If you ask for God's help, He can transform your life. The same God who created the universe will help you defeat the harmful habits that have been holding you back. So, if at first you don't succeed, keep praying. God is listening, and He's ready to help you accomplish your goals if you ask Him. So ask. Today.

More FROM GOD'S WORD

*Dear friend, I pray that you may prosper in every way
and be in good health, just as you are spiritually.*

III JOHN 1:2 HCSB

*Who is wise and has understanding among you?
He should show his works by good conduct with wisdom's gentleness.*

JAMES 3:13 HCSB

Do not be deceived: "Bad company corrupts good morals."

I CORINTHIANS 15:33 HCSB

*Be sober! Be on the alert! Your adversary the Devil is prowling
around like a roaring lion, looking for anyone he can devour.*

I PETER 5:8 HCSB

*Don't you yourselves know that you are God's sanctuary
and that the Spirit of God lives in you?*

I CORINTHIANS 3:16 HCSB

About Habits

We first make our habits, then our habits make us.

JOHN DRYDEN

If you want to form a new habit, get to work.
If you want to break a bad habit, get on your knees.

MARIE T. FREEMAN

God is voting for us all the time. The Devil is voting
against us all the time. The way we vote carries the election.

CORRIE TEN BOOM

Every day, I find countless opportunities to decide whether
I will obey God and demonstrate my love for Him or try to
please myself or the world system. God is waiting for my choices.

BILL BRIGHT

Habits are like a cable. We weave a strand
every day and soon it cannot be broken.

HORACE MANN

FOOD TIP
Make Good Use of Your Downtime

When you find yourself with free time, don't automatically reach for the clicker or for your smartphone. Instead, get up and move around. Try doing stretches when you're bored instead of checking your phone. Or, if you have enough time, take a walk.

FITNESS TIP
First You Make Your Habits. Then Your Habits Make You.

Life is a gift—health must be earned. We earn good health by cultivating healthy habits. The only way that you'll revolutionize your physical health is to revolutionize your habits. The sooner you start acquiring those healthier habits, the better.

TODAY'S FOCUS

Make a list of any unhealthy habits that you need to correct. Then, write down the benefits of establishing new, healthier habits.

7

YOUR OWN PERSONAL PLAN

The wise see danger ahead and avoid it,
but fools keep going and get into trouble.

PROVERBS 22:3 NCV

If you're like most people, you probably have some sort of informal master plan for your life, a general idea of where you want to go and how you expect to get there. But sometimes, informal plans aren't enough. Savvy men and women understand—and the Bible makes it clear—that careful planning pays impressive dividends while impulsive decision-making often does not.

Do you have a fitness plan that includes a healthy diet and regular exercise? Is that plan written down? And are you keeping a daily record of your progress? If so, you've improved your chances of success. So if you haven't already done so, pray about your plans, commit them to writing, and commit them to God. Then, get busy, get excited, and get ready to reap the bountiful harvest that He most certainly has in store.

More FROM GOD'S WORD

But a noble person plans noble things;
he stands up for noble causes.

ISAIAH 32:8 HCSB

A wise man will listen and increase his learning,
and a discerning man will obtain guidance.

PROVERBS 1:5 HCSB

So prepare your minds for action and exercise self-control.
Put all your hope in the gracious salvation that will come
to you when Jesus Christ is revealed to the world.

I PETER 1:13 NLT

Trust in the LORD with all your heart, and lean not
on your own understanding; in all your ways acknowledge Him,
and He shall direct your paths.

PROVERBS 3:5–6 NKJV

Let your eyes look forward; fix your gaze straight ahead.

PROVERBS 4:25 HCSB

About Your Plans

*It is important to set goals because if you do not have a plan,
a goal, a direction, a purpose, and a focus, you are not
going to accomplish anything for the glory of God.*

Bill Bright

*The only way you can experience abundant life
is to surrender your plans to Him.*

Charles Stanley

Attention to little things is a great thing.

St. John Chrysostom

A goal properly set is halfway reached.

Zig Ziglar

*When obstacles arise, you change your direction to reach
your goal; you do not change your decision to get there.*

Zig Ziglar

Food Tip

Whole-Grain Shoppers Beware

Whole grains are great for you, but don't fall for clever marketing gimmicks. "Multigrain," "100% wheat," or "7-grain" products aren't necessarily 100% whole-grain products and may not contain any whole grain at all.

Fitness Tip

Give Your Body the Respect It Deserves

God has given you a body, and He's placed you in charge of caring for it. Your body is, indeed, a temple that should be treated with respect.

Today's Focus

Think about steps you can take right now to begin improving your fitness, your stamina, and your overall health.

8

It's All about Moderation

Moderation is better than muscle,
self-control better than political power.

PROVERBS 16:32 MSG

Would you like to immediately improve the quality of your health and your life? Then here's a simple, time-tested formula: learn to curb your appetite and harness your impulses. In other words, learn the wisdom of moderation.

When we learn to temper our appetites, our desires, and our impulses, we are blessed, in part, because God has created a world in which temperance is rewarded and intemperance is inevitably punished.

Moderation is easy, at least in theory. But in practice, it can be much more difficult to abstain from the cornucopia of temptations to be found in an insatiable society such as ours. Yet the rewards of moderation, which are numerous and long-lasting, are always worth the sacrifices required to attain them. So claim your rewards today.

Of course, no one can force you to moderate your appetite. The decision to live temperately (and wisely) is yours and yours alone. And so, by the way, are the consequences.

More FROM GOD'S WORD

Be on your guard, so that your minds are not dulled
from carousing, drunkenness, and worries of life . . .

LUKE 21:34 HCSB

Do what is right and good in the LORD's sight, so that you
may prosper and so that you may enter and possess the good
land the LORD your God swore to [give] your fathers.

DEUTERONOMY 6:18 HCSB

Teach me, O LORD, the way of Your statutes,
and I shall observe it to the end.

PSALM 119:33 NASB

I discipline my body and bring it under strict control, so that
after preaching to others, I myself will not be disqualified.

I CORINTHIANS 9:27 HCSB

Don't associate with those who drink too much wine,
or with those who gorge themselves on meat.
For the drunkard and the glutton will become poor,
and grogginess will clothe [them] in rags.

PROVERBS 23:20–21 HCSB

About Moderation

*Virtue, even attempted virtue, brings light;
indulgence brings fog.*

C. S. Lewis

*Glorify things of the spirit and keep
the things of the flesh under control.*

Nannie Burroughs

The first lesson in Christ's school is self-denial.

Matthew Henry

*If your desires be endless,
your cares and fears will be so too.*

Thomas Fuller

Food Tip

Be Moderate, Be Consistent

Adopt healthy habits you can stick with. In other words,
don't starve yourself. Be moderate, even in your moderation.

Fitness Tip

Everything in excess is opposed to nature.

Hippocrates

Today's Focus

Think about the benefits of a sensible diet
and the costs of an unhealthy diet.

9

GOD WILL HELP

Nevertheless God, who comforts the downcast, comforted us . . .

II CORINTHIANS 7:6 NKJV

God has a plan for every facet of your life, and His plan includes provisions for your spiritual, physical, and emotional health. But He expects you to do your fair share of the work. In a world that is chock-full of tasty temptations and ubiquitous time-wasters, you may find it all too easy to make unhealthy choices. Your challenge, of course, is to resist those unhealthy choices by every means you can, including prayer. And you can be sure that whenever you ask for God's help, He will give it.

God's Word promises that He will support you in good times and comfort you in hard times. The Creator of the universe stands ready to give you the strength to meet any challenge and the courage to accomplish your goals. When you ask for God's help, He responds in His own way and at His own appointed hour. But make no mistake: He always responds.

Today, as you encounter the inevitable challenges of everyday life, remember that your Heavenly Father never leaves you, not even for a moment. He's always available, always ready to listen, always ready to lead. When you make a habit of talking to Him early and often, He'll guide you and comfort you every day of your life.

More FROM GOD'S WORD

*My grace is sufficient for you,
for my power is made perfect in weakness.*

II CORINTHIANS 12:9 NIV

*Therefore humble yourselves under the mighty hand of God,
that He may exalt you in due time,
casting all your care upon Him, for He cares for you.*

I PETER 5:6–7 NKJV

*The LORD is my light and my salvation—
whom should I fear? The LORD is the stronghold of my life—
of whom should I be afraid?*

PSALM 27:1 HCSB

*The LORD is my shepherd; I shall not want.
He makes me to lie down in green pastures;
He leads me beside the still waters. He restores my soul.*

PSALM 23:1–3 NKJV

*Therefore, we may boldly say: The LORD is my helper;
I will not be afraid. What can man do to me?*

HEBREWS 13:6 HCSB

ABOUT GOD'S SUPPORT

Put your hand into the hand of God.
He gives the calmness and serenity of heart and soul.

LETTIE COWMAN

Measure the size of the obstacles
against the size of God.

BETH MOORE

When once we are assured that God is good,
then there can be nothing left to fear.

HANNAH WHITALL SMITH

The will of God is either a burden
we carry or a power which carries us.

CORRIE TEN BOOM

The Lord God of heaven and earth, the Almighty Creator,
He who holds the universe in His hand as though it were
a very little thing, He is your Shepherd, and He has charged
Himself with the care and keeping of you.

HANNAH WHITALL SMITH

FOOD TIP

Start with Soup

A recent study revealed that people who began their biggest meal of the day with a low-calorie vegetable soup consumed 20 percent fewer calories than before. Give it a try and see if it works for you.

FITNESS TIP

Have Faith and Do the Work

Here's a proven formula for success: have faith in God and do the work. It has been said that there are no shortcuts to any place worth going, and those words apply to your physical fitness too. There are simply no shortcuts to a healthy lifestyle.

TODAY'S FOCUS

Think about what it means to be loved and protected by God.

10

SUSTAINABLE EXERCISE

*But I discipline my body and bring it into subjection,
lest, when I have preached to others,
I myself should become disqualified.*

I CORINTHIANS 9:27 NKJV

Physical fitness is a choice, a choice that requires discipline. Understanding the need for discipline is easy, but leading a disciplined life can be hard. Why? Because it's usually more fun to eat a second piece of cake than it is to jog a second lap around the track. Nonetheless, as we survey the second helpings that all too often find their way on to our plates, we should consider this: as Christians, we are instructed to lead disciplined lives, and when we behave in undisciplined ways, we are living outside of God's will.

We live in a world in which leisure is glorified and consumption is commercialized. But God has other plans. He did not create us for lives of laziness or gluttony; He created us for greater things.

God has a plan for every aspect of your life, and His plan includes provisions for your physical health. His plan probably includes regular, sustainable exercise. Given that fact, you're faced with a dilemma. To paraphrase Hamlet, "To exercise or not to exercise. That is the question." The answer should be obvious.

More FROM GOD'S WORD

*Do you not know that you are the temple of God
and that the Spirit of God dwells in you?*

I CORINTHIANS 3:16 NKJV

*He makes the whole body fit together perfectly. As each part
does its own special work, it helps the other parts grow,
so that the whole body is healthy and growing and full of love.*

EPHESIANS 4:16 NLT

*For I will restore health unto thee,
and I will heal thee of thy wounds, saith the LORD.*

JEREMIAH 30:17 KJV

*I shall yet praise him, who is the health
of my countenance, and my God.*

PSALM 42:11 KJV

*I'm staying alert and in top condition.
I'm not going to get caught napping, telling everyone else
all about it and then missing out myself.*

I CORINTHIANS 9:27 MSG

About Exercise

To enjoy the glow of good health,
you must exercise.

GENE TUNNEY

Give at least two hours every day to exercise,
for health must not be sacrificed to learning.
A strong body makes the mind strong.

THOMAS JEFFERSON

An early morning walk
is a blessing for the whole day.

HENRY DAVID THOREAU

The reason I exercise
is for the quality of life I enjoy.

KENNETH H. COOPER

FOOD TIP

Keep Healthy Snacks Nearby

If you have an apple in your handbag or an orange in your backpack, you'll be less likely to reach for a candy bar or a bag of chips.

FITNESS TIP

Walking is man's best medicine.

HIPPOCRATES

TODAY'S FOCUS

Focus on the long-term benefits of regular, sensible exercise.

11

THE RIGHT ATTITUDE

Finally, brothers, rejoice. Be restored,
be encouraged, be of the same mind, be at peace,
and the God of love and peace will be with you.

II CORINTHIANS 13:11 HCSB

If you're serious about improving your physical, emotional, or spiritual health, it helps to have a positive attitude. Attitudes are the mental filters through which we view and interpret the world around us. People with positive attitudes look for the best, expect the best, and usually find it. People burdened by chronically negative attitudes are not so fortunate. They often sabotage their own efforts; because they expect to fail, they unintentionally bring about the results they fear.

Your attitude will inevitably determine the quality and direction of your day and your life. That's why it's so important to stay positive. So how will you direct your thoughts today? Will you hold fast to His promises and expect Him to help you accomplish your goals? Or will you allow your thoughts to be hijacked by negativity and doubt? If you're a thoughtful believer, you'll think optimistically about yourself, your health, and your future. And while you're at it, you'll give thanks to the Creator for more blessings than you can count.

More FROM GOD'S WORD

A merry heart makes a cheerful countenance . . .

PROVERBS 15:13 NKJV

Be glad and rejoice,
because your reward is great in heaven.

MATTHEW 5:12 HCSB

Rejoice always; pray without ceasing.

I THESSALONIANS 5:16–17 NASB

This is the day the LORD has made;
let us rejoice and be glad in it.

PSALM 118:24 HCSB

You must have the same attitude
that Christ Jesus had.

PHILIPPIANS 2:5 NLT

ABOUT YOUR ATTITUDE

Developing a positive attitude means working continually to find what is uplifting and encouraging.

BARBARA JOHNSON

Your attitude, not your aptitude, will determine your altitude.

ZIG ZIGLAR

The longer I live, the more convinced I become that life is 10 percent what happens to us and 90 percent how we respond to it.

CHARLES SWINDOLL

We choose what attitudes we have right now. And it's a continuing choice.

JOHN MAXWELL

The things we think are the things that feed our souls. If we think on pure and lovely things, we shall grow pure and lovely like them; and the converse is equally true.

HANNAH WHITALL SMITH

Food Tip

Eat Before Going to a Party or an Event

If you're invited to an event where lots of high-calorie food is going to be served, don't arrive hungry. Instead, fill yourself up with a few healthy snacks before the big event.

Fitness Tip

Exercise Improves Attitude

Need some smiles? Get active! Exercise improves your mood and your self-esteem, and it gets you in shape at the same time.

Today's Focus

Think about the benefits of maintaining a positive attitude about your health.

12

YOUR BODY, YOUR RESPONSIBILITY

So then, each of us will give an account of himself to God.

ROMANS 14:12 HCSB

God's Word encourages us to take responsibility for our actions, but the world tempts us to do otherwise. The media tries to convince us that we're "victims" of our upbringing, our urges, our economic strata, our habits, or our circumstances, thus ignoring the countless blessings—and the gift of free will—that God has given each of us.

Who's responsible for your body, your fitness, and your diet? God's Word says that you are. If you obey His instructions and follow His Son, you'll be blessed in countless ways. But if you ignore the Lord's teachings, you must eventually bear the consequences of those irresponsible decisions.

Today and every day, as you make decisions about the things you eat and the way you treat your body, remember who's responsible. The blame game has no winners, so don't play.

More FROM GOD'S WORD

But each person should examine his own work,
and then he will have a reason for boasting in himself alone,
and not in respect to someone else.
For each person will have to carry his own load.

GALATIANS 6:4–5 HCSB

Then He said to His disciples,
"The harvest is abundant,
but the workers are few."

MATTHEW 9:37 HCSB

Wherefore by their fruits ye shall know them.

MATTHEW 7:20 KJV

We must do the works of Him who sent Me
while it is day. Night is coming when no one can work.

JOHN 9:4 HCSB

Better to be patient than powerful;
better to have self-control than to conquer a city.

PROVERBS 16:32 NLT

About Responsibility

Action springs not from thought,
but from a readiness for responsibility.

DIETRICH BONHOEFFER

We talk about circumstances that are
"beyond our control." None of us have control
over our circumstances, but we are responsible
for the way we pilot ourselves in the midst of things as they are.

OSWALD CHAMBERS

Man must cease attributing his problems to his environment,
and learn again to exercise his will—his personal responsibility
in the realm of faith and morals.

ALBERT SCHWEITZER

Firmly entrenched within every human being lies
a most deceptive presupposition: that circumstances and other
people are responsible for our own responses in life.

ERWIN LUTZER

Faithfulness in carrying out present duties
is the best preparation for the future.

FRANÇOIS FÈNELON

FOOD TIP

At Fast-Food Establishments, Choose the Healthier Options

Today, most restaurants offer healthier options for health-conscious patrons. When in doubt, pick the healthier choice. In other words, order the fruit instead of the fries.

FITNESS TIP

Don't Play the Blame Game

If you're fighting the battle of the bulge (the bulging waistline, that is), don't waste time blaming the fast-food industry, the candy manufacturers, or anybody else, for that matter. It's your body, and it's your responsibility to take care of it.

TODAY'S FOCUS

Think about the importance of taking full responsibility for the foods you choose to eat.

13

BE GRATEFUL FOR YOUR BODY, TAKE CARE OF YOUR BODY

*Enter into His gates with thanksgiving, and into His courts
with praise. Be thankful to Him, and bless His name.
For the LORD is good; His mercy is everlasting,
and His truth endures to all generations.*

PSALM 100:4–5 NKJV

Each of us has much to be thankful for. We all have more blessings than we can count, beginning with the precious gift of life. Every good gift comes from our Father above, and we owe Him our never-ending thanks. But sometimes, when the demands of everyday life press down upon us, we neglect to express our gratitude to the Creator.

Your body is an amazing gift, entrusted to you by the Father. When you treat that gift with the care and respect it deserves, you'll be blessed. By caring for your body, you're demonstrating real appreciation for God's gift.

The Lord loves us; He cares for us; He has a plan for each of us; and He has offered us the gift of eternal life through His Son. Considering all the things the Lord has done, we should slow down many times each day and offer our thanks. His grace is everlasting; our thanks should be too.

More FROM GOD'S WORD

And whatever you do, in word or in deed,
do everything in the name of the Lord Jesus,
giving thanks to God the Father through Him.

COLOSSIANS 3:17 HCSB

Surely the righteous shall give thanks to Your name;
The upright shall dwell in Your presence.

PSALM 140:13 NKJV

I will thank the LORD with all my heart;
I will declare all Your wonderful works.
I will rejoice and boast about You;
I will sing about Your name, Most High.

PSALM 9:1–2 HCSB

Thanks be to God for His indescribable gift.

II CORINTHIANS 9:15 HCSB

Rejoice always, pray without ceasing,
in everything give thanks;
for this is the will of God in Christ Jesus for you.

I THESSALONIANS 5:16–18 NKJV

About Gratitude

How ridiculous to grasp for future gifts when today's is set before you. Receive today's gift gratefully, unwrapping it tenderly and delving into its depths.

Sarah Young

In the ordinary life, we hardly realize that we receive a great deal more than we give, and that it is only with gratitude that life becomes rich.

Dietrich Bonhoeffer

God is in control, and therefore in everything I can give thanks—not because of the situation but because of the One who directs and rules over it.

Kay Arthur

Thanksgiving or complaining—these words express two contrasting attitudes of the souls of God's children. The soul that gives thanks can find comfort in everything; the soul that complains can find comfort in nothing.

Hannah Whitall Smith

Fill up the spare moments of your life with praise and thanksgiving.

Sarah Young

Food Tip

Avoid Diet Sodas

Diet sodas use artificial sweeteners that may be harmful to your
health and may even increase hunger, thus increasing weight.
So, if you're thirsty, drink water, not soda.

Fitness Tip

Consider Your Healthy Lifestyle a Form of Worship

God knew precisely what He was doing when He described
your body as a temple. Maintaining that temple is up to you.

Today's Focus

Your body is God's gift to you. When you respect the gift,
you're demonstrating gratitude to the Giver.

14

BECOME AN EXPERT

Wisdom is the principal thing; therefore get wisdom.
And in all your getting, get understanding.

PROVERBS 4:7 NKJV

If you're serious about establishing healthier habits, you owe it to yourself to acquire a basic knowledge of foods and fitness regimens. Do you need to be a world-class scholar in physiology or a Nobel-caliber chemist? Of course not. But you do need to understand the fundamental principles of healthy living. Thankfully, you live in an information-rich society where food and fitness facts are readily available from a wide range of reputable sources. But a word of warning: not all forms of health-related information are created equal.

Many of the food products that are marketed as "healthy alternatives" are actually junk foods in disguise. And most of the get-fit-fast exercise contraptions that are advertised on late-night TV are merely gimmicks. So beware of advertisers' claims and be appropriately skeptical of slick sales pitches. Instead, rely on the kind of unbiased, well-researched sources that you can find at the local library or (surprise!) online. The information is free, but the benefits might just be priceless.

More FROM GOD'S WORD

Commit yourself to instruction;
listen carefully to words of knowledge.

PROVERBS 23:12 NLT

Joyful is the person who finds wisdom,
the one who gains understanding.

PROVERBS 3:13 NLT

Teach me Your way, Yahweh, and I will live by Your truth.
Give me an undivided mind to fear Your name.

PSALM 86:11 HCSB

Anyone who listens to my teaching and follows it is wise,
like a person who builds a house on solid rock.

MATTHEW 7:24 NLT

Enthusiasm without knowledge is not good.
If you act too quickly, you might make a mistake.

PROVERBS 19:2 NCV

About Lifetime Learning

*I am still learning, for the Christian life
is one of constant growth.*

Billy Graham

*True learning can take place at every age of life,
and it doesn't have to be in the curriculum plan.*

Suzanne Dale Ezell

*A time of trouble and darkness is meant
to teach you lessons you desperately need.*

Lettie Cowman

Learning makes a man fit company for himself.

Thomas Fuller

*Life is not a holiday but an education.
And the one eternal lesson for all of us is how we can love.*

Henry Drummond

Food Tip

It's Not That Complicated

You don't have to have a PhD in nutrition to understand the basic principles of maintaining a healthy lifestyle. In today's information-packed world, there's no excuse for being ill-informed.

Fitness Tip

Getting What You Really Deserve

Instead of telling yourself that you deserve to eat some tasty (but unhealthy) food, tell yourself that you deserve to be healthy, happy, and fit.

Today's Focus

Focus on acquiring knowledge about foods and fitness.

15

CELEBRATE THE GIFT OF LIFE

Rejoice in the Lord always. Again I will say, rejoice!

PHILIPPIANS 4:4 NKJV

Each day contains cause for celebration. And each day has its own share of blessings. Our assignment, as grateful believers, is to look for the blessings and celebrate them.

This day, like every other, is a priceless gift from God. He has offered us yet another opportunity to serve Him with smiling faces and willing hands. When we do our part, He inevitably does His part, and miracles happen.

The Lord has promised to bless you and keep you, now and forever. So, don't wait for birthdays or holidays. Make this day an exciting adventure. And while you're at it, take time to thank God for His blessings. He deserves your gratitude, and you deserve the joy of expressing it.

More from God's Word

A happy heart is like a continual feast.

Proverbs 15:15 NCV

Rejoice always, pray without ceasing,
in everything give thanks;
for this is the will of God in Christ Jesus for you.

I Thessalonians 5:16–18 NKJV

I delight greatly in the Lord;
my soul rejoices in my God.

Isaiah 61:10 NIV

I came that they may have life,
and have it abundantly.

John 10:10 NASB

This is the day which the Lord has made;
Let us rejoice and be glad in it.

Psalm 118:24 NASB

About Celebration

Every day we live is a priceless gift of God, loaded with possibilities to learn something new, to gain fresh insights.

DALE EVANS ROGERS

Instead of living a black-and-white existence, we'll be released into a Technicolor world of vibrancy and emotion when we more accurately reflect His nature to the world around us.

BILL HYBELS

The greatest honor you can give Almighty God is to live gladly and joyfully because of the knowledge of His love.

JULIANA OF NORWICH

All our life is celebration to us. We are convinced, in fact, that God is always everywhere.

ST. CLEMENT OF ALEXANDRIA

There is not one blade of grass, there is no color in this world that is not intended to make us rejoice.

JOHN CALVIN

Food Tip

Too Much Salt Spells Trouble

The average American consumes twice as much salt as is recommended. To cut down on sodium, move the salt shaker off the table and put it in the pantry. Out of sight, out of mind.

Fitness Tip

Think Fitness

Fitness is a state of body, mind, and spirit:
if your mind leads, your body will follow.

Today's Focus

Focus on the things you need to celebrate today and every day.

16

IT TAKES WORK

Whatever you do, do it enthusiastically,
as something done for the Lord and not for men.

COLOSSIANS 3:23 HCSB

If food management were easy, there would be no need for diets. And if exercise were easy, the vast majority of folks would be fit as fiddles. But it doesn't work that way. Sticking to a sensible diet is difficult in a world where calories are cheap and fattening foods are plentiful. And physical exercise is demanding, which is why most people spend more time eyeballing their screens than exercising their bodies.

Attaining physical fitness requires determination and discipline, which is perfectly okay with God. Time and again, His Word extols the value of hard work, and so should we. The Lord has created a world in which labor is rewarded but laziness is not. If we want to accomplish our goals, we must work to achieve them.

God has big plans for you, and He's given you everything you need to fulfill His purpose. But He won't force His plans upon you, and He won't do all the work. He expects you to do your part. When you do, you'll earn the rewards He most certainly has in store.

More FROM GOD'S WORD

But this I say: He who sows sparingly will also reap sparingly,
and he who sows bountifully will also reap bountifully.

II CORINTHIANS 9:6 NKJV

The plans of hard-working people earn a profit,
but those who act too quickly become poor.

PROVERBS 21:5 NCV

Do you see a man skilled in his work?
He will stand in the presence of kings . . .

PROVERBS 22:29 HCSB

I must work the works of Him who sent Me while it is day;
the night is coming when no one can work.

JOHN 9:4 NKJV

Be strong and courageous, and do the work.
Don't be afraid or discouraged, for the LORD God,
my God, is with you. He won't leave you or forsake you.

I CHRONICLES 28:20 HCSB

About Work

God did not intend for us to be idle and unproductive.
There is dignity in work.

BILLY GRAHAM

Work is a blessing. God has so arranged the world that work is
necessary, and He gives us hands and strength to do it.
The enjoyment of leisure would be nothing if we had only leisure.

ELISABETH ELLIOT

It may be that the day of judgment will dawn tomorrow;
in that case, we shall gladly stop working for a better future.
But not before.

DIETRICH BONHOEFFER

Ordinary work, which is what most of us do most of the time,
is ordained by God every bit as much as is the extraordinary.

ELISABETH ELLIOT

Work isn't only earning a living; work gives us a sense
of purpose, and worth, and opportunities for companionship.

BILLY GRAHAM

Food Tip

Home-Cooked Can Be Healthier

When you can, cook your own meal instead of ordering takeout
so you can control the ingredients and the portion size.

Fitness Tip

Water Works

Too hot outside for a walk or a jog? Try taking
a swim at the local pool or community center.
Swimming is terrific, low-impact exercise.

Today's Focus

Take time to focus on the rewards you'll earn as you do
the hard work required to improve your physical fitness.

17

Getting Enough Rest?

*Come unto me, all ye that labor and are heavy laden,
and I will give you rest.*

Matthew 11:28 KJV

You inhabit an interconnected world that never slows down and never shuts off. The world tempts you to stay up late watching the news, or surfing the Internet, or checking out social media, or gaming, or doing countless other activities that gobble up your time and distract you from more important tasks. But too much late-night screen time robs you of something you need very badly: sleep.

Are you going to bed at a reasonable hour and sleeping through the night? If so, you're both wise and blessed. But if you're staying up late with your eyes glued to a screen, you're putting your long-term health at risk. And you're probably wasting time too.

So, the next time you're tempted to engage in late-night time-wasting, resist the temptation. Instead, turn your thoughts and prayers to God. And when you're finished, turn off the lights and go to bed. You need rest more than you need entertainment.

More FROM GOD'S WORD

Take My yoke upon you and learn from Me, because I am gentle
and humble in heart, and you will find rest for your souls.
For My yoke is easy and My burden is light.

MATTHEW 11:29–30 HCSB

The LORD shall give thee rest from thy sorrow,
and from thy fear . . .

ISAIAH 14:3 KJV

In quietness and in confidence shall be your strength . . .

ISAIAH 30:15 KJV

Finally, brothers, rejoice. Become mature,
be encouraged, be of the same mind, be at peace,
and the God of love and peace will be with you.

II CORINTHIANS 13:11 HCSB

Return unto thy rest, O my soul;
for the LORD hath dealt bountifully with thee.

PSALM 116:7 KJV

About Rest

Life is strenuous. See that your clock does not run down.

LETTIE COWMAN

Prescription for a happier and healthier life:
resolve to slow your pace; learn to say no gracefully;
reject the temptation to chase after more pleasures,
more hobbies, and more social entanglements.

JAMES DOBSON

You live among people who glorify busyness.
They've made time a tyrant that controls their lives.

SARAH YOUNG

He who cannot rest, cannot work; he who cannot let go,
cannot hold on; he who cannot find footing, cannot go forward.

HARRY EMERSON FOSDICK

The more comfortable we are with mystery in our journey,
the more rest we will know along the way.

JOHN ELDREDGE

Food Tip
Strive for Whole Grains, Not Refined

Try to replace half of the refined grains on your plate (think bread, pasta, and rice) with whole grains. Whole grains are a good source of fiber and other important nutrients.

Fitness Tip
Sleep Is Essential

Don't underestimate the power of sleep. It's healthiest to be on a regular routine, so try getting to bed at the same time every night and waking up with your alarm in the morning.

Today's Focus

Think about what it would take—and what changes you might need to make—in order to get eight hours of sleep each night.

18

REGULAR CHECKUPS

The wise are glad to be instructed . . .

PROVERBS 10:8 NLT

Do you have a personal physician, and do you see your doctor for regular checkups? If so, feel free to skip to the next page. But if you can't remember the last time you had a checkup, please keep reading.

Even if you feel perfectly fine, even if you haven't had pain in years, even if you're the picture of health, as healthy as a horse, or any other idiom you can think of, you still need to see your MD for regularly scheduled physical exams. Modern medicine has given mankind miraculous tools to detect diseases early and cure them completely. But early detection is often the key to successful treatment. So make it a point to see your doctor regularly. You're worth it.

More FROM GOD'S WORD

How much better is it to get wisdom than gold!
and to get understanding rather to be chosen than silver!

PROVERBS 16:16 KJV

He whose ear listens to the life-giving reproof
will dwell among the wise.

PROVERBS 15:31 NASB

Get all the advice and instruction you can,
so you will be wise the rest of your life.

PROVERBS 19:20 NLT

Get wisdom—how much better it is than gold!
And get understanding—it is preferable to silver.

PROVERBS 16:16 HCSB

Plans fail when there is no counsel,
but with many advisers they succeed.

PROVERBS 15:22 HCSB

Getting (and Taking) Good Advice

If a man knows where to get good advice,
it is as though he could supply it himself.

Johann Wolfgang von Goethe

It takes a wise person to give good advice,
but an even wiser person to take it.

Marie T. Freeman

Calisthenics can build up the body. Courses of study
can train the mind. But the real champion
is the person whose heart can be educated.

Fred Russell

To accept good advice is but to increase one's own ability.

Johann Wolfgang von Goethe

Know or listen to those who know.

Baltasar Gracián

FOOD TIP
Focus on DV (Daily Value)

Looking for some food-label magic? Check out the
"Daily Value" column. Generally speaking, 5 percent DV or less
is low, while 20 percent DV or more is high.

FITNESS TIP
Trust God's Guidebook

The Bible is full of advice about health, moderation,
and sensible living. When you come across these passages,
take them to heart and put them to use.

TODAY'S FOCUS

Spend a few moments considering the
miraculous benefits of modern medicine.

19

ALL THINGS ARE POSSIBLE

But Jesus looked at them and said to them,
"With men this is impossible,
but with God all things are possible."

MATTHEW 19:26 NKJV

Are you secretly afraid that you simply don't have what it takes to achieve a higher level of physical fitness? If so, please remember this: with God, all things are possible.

God has put you in a particular place, at a specific time of His choosing. He has an assignment that is uniquely yours, tasks that are specially intended just for you. And whether you know it or not, He's equipped you with everything you need to fulfill His purpose and achieve His plans.

So the next time you find yourself stuck in the quicksand of self-doubt, refocus your thoughts and redouble your prayers. Then, turn everything over to the Lord. When you let Him take over, there's simply no limit to the things that the two of you, working together, can accomplish.

More FROM GOD'S WORD

I can do all things through
Christ which strengtheneth me.

PHILIPPIANS 4:13 KJV

The things which are impossible with men
are possible with God.

LUKE 18:27 KJV

Therefore we do not lose heart.
Even though our outward man is perishing,
yet the inward man is being renewed day by day.

II CORINTHIANS 4:16 NKJV

Is anything too hard for the LORD?

GENESIS 18:14 KJV

Jesus said to him, "If you can believe,
all things are possible to him who believes."

MARK 9:23 NKJV

About Possibilities

*God's specialty is raising dead things to life
and making impossible things possible.
You don't have the need that exceeds His power.*

BETH MOORE

*I have found that there are three stages
in every great work of God: first, it is impossible,
then it is difficult, then it is done.*

HUDSON TAYLOR

*We are all faced with a series of great opportunities
brilliantly disguised as impossible situations.*

CHARLES SWINDOLL

*Alleged "impossibilities" are opportunities
for our capacities to be stretched.*

CHARLES SWINDOLL

A possibility is a hint from God.

SØREN KIERKEGAARD

FOOD TIP

Focus on Nutrition

When shopping for healthy food, make your calories count.
But be sure to strike a balance with nutrition. Try to find foods
with the most nutrients for a given number of calories.

FITNESS TIP

Train Yourself to Think and Speak Positively about Your Health and Your Diet

The words you use impact your thoughts and your
thoughts have a way of becoming reality. So, instead
of using words like *fat*, say *fit*; change *I can't* to *I can*;
change *helpless* to *strong*. You get the idea.

TODAY'S FOCUS

Think about God's power to help you bring
about miraculous changes in your life.

20

DON'T GIVE UP

*Let us not become weary in doing good, for at the proper time
we will reap a harvest if we do not give up.*

GALATIANS 6:9 NIV

Occasionally, good things happen with little or no effort. Somebody inherits a fortune, or wins the lottery, or stumbles onto a financial bonanza by being at the right place at the right time. But more often than not, good things happen to people who work hard and keep working hard.

Calvin Coolidge observed, "Nothing in the world can take the place of persistence. Talent will not; genius will not; education will not. Persistence and determination alone are omnipotent." And President Coolidge was right. Perseverance pays.

So when it comes to your physical, emotional, or spiritual fitness, don't give up and don't give in. Just keep putting one foot in front of the other, pray for strength, live in day-tight compartments, and keep going. Whether you realize it or not, you're up to the challenge if you persevere. And with God's help, that's exactly what you'll do.

More FROM GOD'S WORD

*But as for you, be strong; don't be discouraged,
for your work has a reward.*

II CHRONICLES 15:7 HCSB

*Finishing is better than starting.
Patience is better than pride.*

ECCLESIASTES 7:8 NLT

*For you have need of endurance,
so that when you have done the will of God,
you may receive what was promised.*

HEBREWS 10:36 NASB

*So let us run the race that is before us and never give up.
We should remove from our lives anything that would
get in the way and the sin that so easily holds us back.*

HEBREWS 12:1 NCV

*We are hard-pressed on every side, yet not crushed;
we are perplexed, but not in despair.*

II CORINTHIANS 4:8 NKJV

About Perseverance

Perseverance is more than endurance.
It is endurance combined with
absolute assurance and certainty
that what we are looking for is going to happen.

Oswald Chambers

Perseverance is not a passive submission
to circumstances—it is a strong a
nd active response to the difficult events of life.

Elizabeth George

Success or failure can be pretty well predicted
by the degree to which the heart is fully in it.

John Eldredge

Patience and diligence, like faith, remove mountains.

William Penn

Everyone gets discouraged. The question is:
Are you going to give up or get up? It's a choice.

John Maxwell

FOOD TIP

When You Eat a Treat, Take Your Time

When you're eating a well-deserved treat, don't gobble it down.
Take your time. When you slow down and think about what
you're eating, you'll feel more satisfied.

FITNESS TIP

*No amount of falls will really undo us
if we keep picking ourselves up after each one.*

C. S. LEWIS

TODAY'S FOCUS

Think about the rewards of perseverance
and the cost of giving up too soon.

21

PRAY ABOUT IT

Rejoice always, pray without ceasing,
in everything give thanks;
for this is the will of God in Christ Jesus for you.

I THESSALONIANS 5:16–18 NKJV

Prayer is a powerful tool that you can use to change your world and change yourself. God hears every prayer and responds in His own way and according to His own timetable. When you make a habit of consulting Him about everything, He'll guide you along a path of His choosing, which, by the way, is the path you should take. And when you petition Him for strength, He'll give you the courage to face any problem and the power to meet any challenge.

So today, instead of turning things over in your mind, turn them over to God in prayer. Take your concerns about fitness, food, and faith—or just about anything else for that matter—to the Lord. He's always ready to listen and always willing to help. The rest is up to you.

More FROM GOD'S WORD

*I desire therefore that the men pray everywhere,
lifting up holy hands, without wrath and doubting.*

I TIMOTHY 2:8 NKJV

*Confess your trespasses to one another, and pray for one another,
that you may be healed. The effective,
fervent prayer of a righteous man avails much.*

JAMES 5:16 NKJV

*And whenever you stand praying, if you have
anything against anyone, forgive him, so that your
Father in heaven may also forgive you your wrongdoing.*

MARK 11:25 HCSB

*Ask, and it shall be given to you; seek, and you shall find;
knock, and it shall be opened to you. For every one
who asks receives, and he who seeks finds,
and to him who knocks it shall be opened.*

MATTHEW 7:7–8 NASB

Is anyone among you suffering? He should pray.

JAMES 5:13 HCSB

About Prayer

Prayer is our lifeline to God.

Billy Graham

*Any concern that is too small
to be turned into a prayer is too small
to be made into a burden.*

Corrie ten Boom

*It is impossible to overstate the need for prayer
in the fabric of family life.*

James Dobson

*Don't pray when you feel like it.
Have an appointment with the Lord and keep it.*

Corrie ten Boom

*Two wings are necessary to lift our souls toward God:
prayer and praise. Prayer asks. Praise accepts the answer.*

Lettie Cowman

FOOD TIP
Eat Lots of Fiber

Foods containing lots of fiber will make you
feel fuller faster. Plus, fiber is essential to good
digestive health. So when in doubt, eat more fiber.

FITNESS TIP
Stretch!

Try basic stretches before vigorous exercising—
especially sports—to avoid muscle injuries. But be sure
to stretch safely! If you feel pain, you've gone too far.

TODAY'S FOCUS

Think about the power of prayer. And think about
ways that you can improve your prayer life.

22

THE RIGHT PRIORITIES

*Therefore, whether you eat or drink,
or whatever you do, do everything for God's glory.*

1 CORINTHIANS 10:31 HCSB

What are your priorities for the coming day and the coming year? Will you focus on your health, your work, your family, or your finances? All these things are important, of course, but God asks you to focus on something entirely different. God asks that you focus not on yourself or your world but on Him.

Every morning, when you rise from bed and prepare for the coming day, the world attempts to arrange your priorities, to fill your schedule, and to crowd out God. The world says you're too busy to pray, too busy to study God's Word, and too busy to thank Him for His gifts. The world says you need noise instead of silence, entertainment instead of contemplation, constant contact instead of solitude. And the world says that you'll stay on the right track if you simply do enough and acquire enough. But God begs to differ. He asks that you quiet yourself each day and listen to Him. And He promises that when you listen, He will lead.

So, as you think about the things in your life that really matter— and as you establish priorities for the coming day—remember to let God lead the way. And while you're at it, remember that the things that matter most are always the things that have eternal consequences.

More FROM GOD'S WORD

*Trust in the L*ORD *with all your heart
and lean not on your own understanding.*

PROVERBS 3:5 NIV

*But prove yourselves doers of the word,
and not merely hearers who delude themselves.*

JAMES 1:22 NASB

*For where your treasure is,
there your heart will be also.*

LUKE 12:34 HCSB

*He who trusts in his riches will fall,
but the righteous will flourish.*

PROVERBS 11:28 NASB

*Set an example of good works yourself,
with integrity and dignity in your teaching.*

TITUS 2:7 HCSB

ABOUT PRIORITIES

Energy and time are limited entities. Therefore, we need to use them wisely, focusing on what is truly important.

SARAH YOUNG

Great relief and satisfaction can come from seeking God's priorities for us in each season, discerning what is "best" in the midst of many noble opportunities, and pouring our most excellent energies into those things.

BETH MOORE

Put first things first and we get second things thrown in; put second things first and we lose both first and second things.

ELIZABETH GEORGE

A disciple is a follower of Christ. That means you take on His priorities as your own. His agenda becomes your agenda. His mission becomes your mission.

CHARLES STANLEY

Each day is God's gift of a fresh, unspoiled opportunity to live according to His priorities.

ELIZABETH GEORGE

FOOD TIP

Occasional Treats Are Okay, But in Moderation

There's no reason you can't enjoy an occasional treat if you can maintain a healthy diet and stay within your daily calorie allowance. But don't overdo it. And if you find yourself binging, stop altogether.

FITNESS TIP

God's Promises Never Fail

Never lose sight of God's promises. His guidebook,
the Holy Bible, contains eternal truths that offer
you courage, hope, and health. Trust God's promises.

TODAY'S FOCUS

Think about your highest priorities. Are you
spending enough time on top priorities?

23

IT TAKES DISCIPLINE

Discipline yourself for the purpose of godliness.

I TIMOTHY 4:7 NASB

It takes discipline to attain a higher level of physical fitness. God does not reward apathy, laziness, or idleness, nor does He reward undisciplined behavior. To the contrary, the Lord expects us to lead disciplined lives despite worldly temptations to do otherwise.

The media glorifies leisure. The ultimate goal, so the message goes, is to win the lottery and then retire to some sunny paradise sitting idly by watching the waves splash onto the sand. Such leisure activities are fine for a few days, but not for a lifetime.

Life's greatest accomplishments are seldom the result of luck. More often than not, our greatest accomplishments require plenty of preparation and lots of work, which is perfectly fine with God. After all, He knows that we can do the work, and He knows the rewards that we'll earn when we finish the job. Besides, God knows that He will always help us complete the tasks He has set before us. As a matter of fact, God usually does at least half the work: the second half.

More FROM GOD'S WORD

Whatever you do, do your work heartily,
as for the Lord rather than for men.

COLOSSIANS 3:23 NASB

But the fruit of the Spirit is love, joy,
peace, patience, kindness, goodness, faith, gentleness,
self-control. Against such things there is no law.

GALATIANS 5:22–23 HCSB

Finishing is better than starting.
Patience is better than pride.

ECCLESIASTES 7:8 NLT

A final word: Be strong with the Lord's mighty power.

EPHESIANS 6:10 NLT

It is better to be patient than powerful;
it is better to have self-control than to conquer a city.

PROVERBS 16:32 NLT

About Discipline

Think of something you ought to do and go do it.
Heed not your feelings. Do your work.

GEORGE MACDONALD

Diligence is the mother of good luck,
and God gives all things to industry.

BEN FRANKLIN

No horse gets anywhere until he is harnessed.
No stream or gas drives anything until it is confined.
No life ever grows great until it is focused, dedicated, disciplined.

HARRY EMERSON FOSDICK

So, let us work hard but never forget that it is not us,
but the grace of God, which is with us.

JOHN PIPER

Personal discipline is a most powerful character quality
and one worthy of dedicating your life to nurturing.

ELIZABETH GEORGE

FOOD TIP
Don't Stock Junk Food

To avoid temptation, don't fill your pantry with unhealthy snack foods and desserts. Stock up on healthy snacks instead.

FITNESS TIP
You Can See Them, but Can They See You?

Exercising outside after dark? Be sure to wear bright, reflective clothes so that you can be seen by the cars around you.

TODAY'S FOCUS

Think about tangible steps you can take
to lead a more disciplined life.

24

THE BALANCING ACT

*I leave you peace; my peace I give you. I do not give it to you
as the world does. So don't let your hearts be troubled or afraid.*

JOHN 14:27 NCV

Life is a delicate balancing act, a tightrope walk with over-commitment on one side and under-commitment on the other. It's up to each of us to walk carefully on that rope, not falling prey to pride (which causes us to attempt too much) or to fear (which causes us to attempt too little).

God has plans for every human being, including you. He has a unique set of tasks that are designed especially for you. Your challenge is to discern His will, as best as you can, and to seek the path that He has chosen for you.

Are you doing too much—or too little? If so, it's time to have a little chat with your Heavenly Father. And if you listen carefully to His instructions, you will strive to achieve a more balanced life, a healthier life, and a life that's right for you and your loved ones. When you do, everybody wins.

More FROM GOD'S WORD

*Abundant peace belongs to those who love Your instruction;
nothing makes them stumble.*

PSALM 119:165 HCSB

But godliness with contentment is a great gain.

I TIMOTHY 6:6 HCSB

*Careful planning puts you ahead in the long run;
hurry and scurry puts you further behind.*

PROVERBS 21:5 MSG

*But those who wait on the LORD
Shall renew their strength;
They shall mount up with wings like eagles,
They shall run and not be weary,
They shall walk and not faint.*

ISAIAH 40:31 NKJV

*Don't burn out; keep yourselves fueled and aflame.
Be alert servants of the Master, cheerfully expectant.
Don't quit in hard times; pray all the harder.*

ROMANS 12:11–12 MSG

About Finding Peace

Deep within the center of the soul is a chamber of peace where God lives and where, if we will enter it and quiet all the other sounds, we can hear His gentle whisper.

LETTIE COWMAN

The knowledge that we are never alone calms the troubled sea of our lives and speaks peace to our souls.

A. W. TOZER

God's peace is like a river, not a pond. In other words, a sense of health and well-being, both of which are expressions of the Hebrew shalom, can permeate our homes even when we're in white-water rapids.

BETH MOORE

Only Christ can meet the deepest needs of our world and our hearts. Christ alone can bring lasting peace.

BILLY GRAHAM

Peace does not mean to be in a place where there is no noise, trouble, or hard work. Peace means to be in the midst of all those things and still be calm in your heart.

CATHERINE MARSHALL

FOOD TIP

Plan Your Meals and Snacks

If you're trying to lose weight, plan your breakfast, lunch, dinner, and snacks for the upcoming week, making sure you stick to your calorie allowance. Then, of course, keep track of your results.

FITNESS TIP

Get Exams, Get Screenings

Ask your health-care provider what exams and tests you need to detect potential health problems before they become big health problems.

TODAY'S FOCUS

Look at your schedule. Are you overcommitted?
If so, consider steps you can take to free up
your schedule and lead a more balanced life.

25

KEEP GROWING

I remind you to fan into flames the spiritual gift God gave you.

II TIMOTHY 1:6 NLT

As a Christian, you should never stop growing. No matter your age, no matter your circumstances, you have opportunities to learn and opportunities to serve. Wherever you happen to be, God is there too, and He wants to bless you with an expanding array of spiritual gifts. Your job is to let Him.

The path to spiritual maturity unfolds day by day. Through prayer, through Bible study, and through obedience to God's Word, we can strengthen our relationship with Him. The more we focus on the Father, the more He blesses our lives.

In the quiet moments when we open our hearts to the Lord, the Creator who made us keeps remaking us. He gives us guidance, perspective, courage, and strength. And the appropriate moment to accept these spiritual gifts is always the present one.

More FROM GOD'S WORD

*But endurance must do its complete work, so that you
may be mature and complete, lacking nothing.*

JAMES 1:4 HCSB

*And be not conformed to this world: but be ye transformed
by the renewing of your mind, that ye may prove
what is that good, and acceptable, and perfect will of God.*

ROMANS 12:2 KJV

*Leave inexperience behind, and you will live;
pursue the way of understanding.*

PROVERBS 9:6 HCSB

*So let us stop going over the basic teachings
about Christ again and again. Let us go on instead
and become mature in our understanding.*

HEBREWS 6:1 NLT

*But grow in the grace and knowledge of our Lord and Savior
Jesus Christ. To Him be the glory both now and forever. Amen.*

II PETER 3:18 NKJV

ABOUT SPIRITUAL GROWTH

Grow, dear friends, but grow, I beseech you,
in God's way, which is the only true way.

HANNAH WHITALL SMITH

We set our eyes on the finish line,
forgetting the past, and straining toward the mark
of spiritual maturity and fruitfulness.

VONETTE BRIGHT

God's ultimate goal for your life on earth is not comfort,
but character development. He wants you
to grow up spiritually and become like Christ.

RICK WARREN

The vigor of our spiritual life will be in exact proportion
to the place held by the Bible in our life and thoughts.

GEORGE MUELLER

Mark it down. You will never go where God is not.

MAX LUCADO

FOOD TIP
Don't Starve Yourself

Consuming too few calories can slow down your metabolism, with harmful results. So eat sensibly every day, but don't starve yourself. A starvation diet is a terrible way to (temporarily) lose weight.

FITNESS TIP
It's a Spiritual Journey Too

View your journey to improved health as both a physical and a spiritual journey. After all, you're taking care of the temple God has entrusted to your care.

TODAY'S FOCUS

Ask God for His guidance as you strive to improve your spiritual, emotional, and physical health.

26

COUNTLESS CHOICES
EVERY DAY

*If you need wisdom—if you want to know what
God wants you to do—ask him, and he will gladly tell you.
He will not rebuke you for asking.*

JAMES 1:5 NLT

Physical fitness is not the result of a single big decision that is made "once and for all." Physical fitness results from thousands of small decisions that are made day after day, week after week, and year after year.

Each day, we make thousands of seemingly insignificant choices concerning the things that we do and the things we think. Most of these choices are made without too much forethought. For many of us, the behaviors that determine our level of fitness are simply the result of impulse or habit. Yet God asks that we slow down long enough to think about the choices that we make, and He asks that we make those choices in accordance with the teachings found in His Holy Word.

More FROM GOD'S WORD

Who is wise and has understanding among you? He should show his works by good conduct with wisdom's gentleness.

JAMES 3:13 HCSB

A good man produces good out of the good storeroom of his heart, and an evil man produces evil out of the evil storeroom. For his mouth speaks from the overflow of the heart.

LUKE 6:45 HCSB

Blessed is the man who walks not in the counsel of the ungodly, nor stands in the path of sinners, nor sits in the seat of the scornful.

PSALM 1:1 NKJV

So you may walk in the way of goodness, and keep to the paths of righteousness. For the upright will dwell in the land, And the blameless will remain in it.

PROVERBS 2:20–21 NKJV

The fear of the LORD is the beginning of knowledge, but fools despise wisdom and discipline.

PROVERBS 1:7 NIV

About Choices

*Your little choices become habits that affect
the bigger decisions you make in life.*

ELIZABETH GEORGE

Every choice you make has an end result.

ZIG ZIGLAR

*How important it is for us—young and old—to live as if Jesus
would return any day—to set our goals, make our choices,
raise our children, and conduct business with
the perspective of the imminent return of our Lord.*

GLORIA GAITHER

*God always gives His very best to those who
leave the choice with Him.*

HUDSON TAYLOR

*There are two great forces at work in the world today:
the unlimited power of God and the limited power of Satan.*

CORRIE TEN BOOM

Food Tip
Eat Only at the Table

Make a habit of sitting at the table when you eat.
Eating at the table can help prevent grazing
and consuming more calories than necessary.

Fitness Tip
Consider Early-Morning Workouts

When you exercise first thing in the morning,
you make certain that, no matter how crazy
the day gets, you've gotten your workout.

Today's Focus

Think about ways that seemingly insignificant,
everyday choices gradually can become habits. And think
about the impact habits have on the quality of your life.

27

HANDLING THE INEVITABLE SETBACKS

*If we confess our sins to him, he is faithful and just
to forgive us and to cleanse us from every wrong.*

1 JOHN 1:9 NLT

As you begin to improve your diet and increase your physical stamina, you'll probably experience a setback or two. Or three. None of us are perfect; we all make mistakes. The question, then, is not whether we'll make mistakes, but what we'll do about them. If we ignore our mistakes, or if we try to cover them up, we invite trouble. But if we learn from our mistakes and make amends whenever possible, God will help us make use of our setbacks.

View every setback as an opportunity to reassess God's will for your life. And while you're at it, consider your mistakes to be powerful opportunities to learn more about yourself, your circumstances, and your world. Everybody (including you) makes mistakes. Your job is to make as few of them as possible. And with God's help, you can do it.

More from God's Word

He who covers his sins will not prosper, but whoever confesses and forsakes them will have mercy.

Proverbs 28:13 NKJV

But the mercy of the Lord is from everlasting to everlasting upon them that fear him, and his righteousness unto children's children . . .

Psalm 103:17 KJV

Be merciful, just as your Father is merciful.

Luke 6:36 NIV

Therefore, if anyone is in Christ, he is a new creation; old things have passed away; behold, all things have become new.

II Corinthians 5:17 NKJV

Therefore let us approach the throne of grace with boldness, so that we may receive mercy and find grace to help us at the proper time.

Hebrews 4:16 HCSB

ABOUT MISTAKES

God is able to take mistakes,
when they are committed to Him,
and make of them something
for our good and for His glory.

RUTH BELL GRAHAM

It is human to err, but it is devilish
to remain willfully in error.

ST. AUGUSTINE

Every misfortune, every failure,
every loss may be transformed.
God has the power to transform
all misfortunes into "God-sends."

LETTIE COWMAN

Mistakes offer the possibility for redemption
and a new start in God's kingdom.
No matter what you're guilty of,
God can restore your innocence.

BARBARA JOHNSON

FOOD TIP

Shop the Perimeter of the Grocery Store

That's where most fresh fruit, veggies, chicken,
fish, eggs, and dairy products are located.
When you go into the center aisles, be sure to take a list.

FITNESS TIP

When You're Too Busy for a Full Workout

It's perfectly okay to settle for a shorter workout.
Some exercise is better than none at all.

TODAY'S FOCUS

Consider the way you react when you make a mistake. Do you
become discouraged and give up, or do you redouble your efforts?

28

PROTECTING YOUR EMOTIONAL HEALTH

*For this very reason, make every effort to supplement your faith
with goodness, goodness with knowledge, knowledge with
self-control, self-control with endurance, endurance with godliness.*

II PETER 1:5–6 HCSB

Emotional health isn't simply the absence of sadness; it's also the ability to enjoy life and celebrate God's gifts.

Christians have every reason to be optimistic about life. But sometimes, when we are tired or frustrated, rejoicing seems only a distant promise. Thankfully, God stands ready to restore us: "I will give you a new heart and put a new spirit in you . . ." (Ezekiel 36:26 NIV). Our task, of course, is to let Him.

If you're feeling deeply discouraged or profoundly depressed, then it is time to seriously address the state of your emotional health. First, open your heart to God in prayer. Then, talk with trusted family members, to friends, and to your pastor. And if you or someone close to you considers it wise, seek advice from your physician or make an appointment with a licensed mental health professional.

When your emotional health is at stake, don't hesitate to ask for help. Then, armed with the promises of your Creator and the support of family and friends, you can go about the business of solving the challenges that confront you. When you do, the clouds will eventually part, and the sun will shine once more upon your soul.

More FROM GOD'S WORD

Grow a wise heart—you'll do yourself a favor;
keep a clear head—you'll find a good life.

PROVERBS 19:8 MSG

And let the peace of God rule in your hearts,
to which also you were called in one body; and be thankful.

COLOSSIANS 3:15 NKJV

Get wisdom—how much better it is than gold!
And get understanding—it is preferable to silver.

PROVERBS 16:16 HCSB

All bitterness, anger and wrath, shouting and slander
must be removed from you, along with all malice.
And be kind and compassionate to one another,
forgiving one another, just as God also forgave you in Christ.

EPHESIANS 4:31–32 HCSB

Enthusiasm without knowledge is not good.
If you act too quickly, you might make a mistake.

PROVERBS 19:2 NCV

About Emotions

Our feelings do not affect God's facts.

Amy Carmichael

It is Christ who is to be exalted, not our feelings.
We will know Him by obedience, not by emotions.
Our love will be shown by obedience,
not by how good we feel about God at a given moment.

Elisabeth Elliot

Our emotions can lie to us,
and we need to counter our emotions with truth.

Billy Graham

Feelings are like chemicals; the more you analyze them,
the worse they smell.

Charles Kingsley

A life lived in God is not lived on the plane of feelings,
but of the will.

Elisabeth Elliot

FOOD TIP

Plan Ahead

If you don't have healthy foods in the house,
you'll be tempted to go out for fast food.
When it comes to healthy eating, it helps to plan ahead.

FITNESS TIP

Workout Clothes Should Be Comfortable, Especially the Shoes

Be sure to wear supportive footwear and comfortable
workout attire. You'll feel better about your exercise.

TODAY'S FOCUS

Focus on the blessings that result from spiritual and emotional health.

29

WHERE TO FIND STRENGTH

He gives strength to the weary,
and to him who lacks might He increases power.

ISAIAH 40:29 NASB

It takes energy to reach your goals. So, where do you turn for strength when you're weary or worried? The medicine cabinet? The gym? The health food store? These places may offer a temporary energy boost, but the best place to find strength and solace isn't down the hall or at the mall; it's as near as your next breath. The best source of strength is God.

God's love for you never changes, and neither does His support. From the cradle to the grave, He has promised to give you the strength to meet the challenges of life. He has promised to guide you and protect you if you let Him. But He also expects you to do your fair share of the work.

Today provides yet another opportunity to partake in the strength that only God can provide. You do so by attuning your heart to Him through prayer, obedience, and trust. Your struggle may be difficult, but fear not. Whatever your challenge, God can give you the strength to face it and to overcome it.

Would you like to become more physically fit? Then start with the firm conviction that God wants the very same thing. And then have faith that when you and God work together, anything is possible.

More FROM GOD'S WORD

The LORD is my strength and my song;
He has become my salvation.

EXODUS 15:2 HCSB

Have faith in the LORD your God, and you will stand strong.
Have faith in his prophets, and you will succeed.

II CHRONICLES 20:20 NCV

Be strong and courageous, and do the work.
Don't be afraid or discouraged, for the LORD God,
my God, is with you. He won't leave you or forsake you.

I CHRONICLES 28:20 HCSB

I can do all things through Christ who strengthens me.

PHILIPPIANS 4:13 NKJV

My grace is sufficient for you,
for my power is made perfect in weakness.

II CORINTHIANS 12:9 NIV

Finding Strength

Faith is a strong power, mastering any difficulty in the strength of the Lord who made heaven and earth.

Corrie ten Boom

God is in control. He may not take away trials or make detours for us, but He strengthens us through them.

Billy Graham

The strength that we claim from God's Word does not depend on circumstances. Circumstances will be difficult, but our strength will be sufficient.

Corrie ten Boom

God will give us the strength and resources we need to live through any situation in life that He ordains.

Billy Graham

The truth is, God's strength is fully revealed when our strength is depleted.

Liz Curtis Higgs

FOOD TIP

Use Smaller Plates

Studies have shown that people who use smaller
plates tend to eat smaller portions and are still satisfied.
By using smaller plates and bowls, you can gradually train
yourself to eat smaller portions without going hungry.

FITNESS TIP

Big Changes Can Start Small

Even walking an extra ten minutes a day is a great
way to start building a healthy fitness routine.

TODAY'S FOCUS

Think about God's strength and what it means to you.

30

ABOVE AND BEYOND WORRY

Therefore do not worry about tomorrow,
for tomorrow will worry about its own things.
Sufficient for the day is its own trouble.

MATTHEW 6:34 NKJV

Because we are human beings who have the capacity to think and to anticipate future events, we worry. Intuitively, we understand that worry damages our health, our relationships, and our ability to accomplish the goals we've set for ourselves. But we worry still.

We worry about big things, little things, and just about everything in between. To make matters worse, we live in a world that breeds anxiety and fosters fear. So it's not surprising that when we come face-to-face with tough times, we may fall prey to discouragement, doubt, or depression. But our Father in heaven has other plans.

God has promised that we may lead lives of abundance, not anxiety. In fact, His Word instructs us to "be anxious for nothing." But how can we put our fears to rest? By taking those fears to Him and leaving them there. The very same God who created the universe has promised to protect you now and forever. So what do you have to worry about? With God on your side, the answer is, "Nothing."

More FROM GOD'S WORD

Let not your heart be troubled;
you believe in God, believe also in Me.

JOHN 14:1 NKJV

Peace I leave with you; My peace I give to you;
not as the world gives do I give to you.
Do not let your heart be troubled, nor let it be fearful.

JOHN 14:27 NASB

Do not be anxious about anything,
but in everything, by prayer and petition,
with thanksgiving, present your requests to God.

PHILIPPIANS 4:6 NIV

Cast your burden on the LORD,
And He shall sustain you;
He shall never permit the righteous to be moved.

PSALM 55:22 NKJV

Cast all your anxiety on him because he cares for you.

I PETER 5:7 NIV

The Futility of Worry

Worry is the senseless process of cluttering up tomorrow's opportunities with leftover problems from today.

BARBARA JOHNSON

Do not worry about tomorrow.
This is not a suggestion, but a command.

SARAH YOUNG

Exchange the bad habit of worrying
with the excellent habit of trusting God.

ELIZABETH GEORGE

Pray, and let God worry.

MARTIN LUTHER

Tomorrow is busy worrying about itself;
don't get tangled up in its worry-webs.

SARAH YOUNG

Food Tip
Consider the Contents of Your Refrigerator

Take a careful look inside your refrigerator. Are the contents reflective of a healthy lifestyle? And if your fridge is overflowing with junk foods, it's time to rethink your shopping habits.

Fitness Tip
Handwashing 101

For fewer colds and better health, wash your hands frequently throughout the day. If soap and water aren't available, use hand sanitizer.

Today's Focus

Make a brief inventory of the things you're most worried about. Then pray for guidance, courage, and the peace that comes from trusting God completely.

31

Asking Him for Help

Ask, and it shall be given to you; seek,
and you shall find; knock, and it shall be opened to you.
For every one who asks receives, and he who seeks finds,
and to him who knocks it shall be opened.

MATTHEW 7:7–8 NASB

Take a few minutes to examine your eating habits. Do you gobble down snack foods while watching television? If so, stop. Do you drink high-calorie soft drinks or feast on unhealthy snacks like potato chips or candy? If so, you're doing yourself a disservice. Do you load up your plate and then feel obligated to eat every last bite? If so, it's time to form some new habits.

Poor eating habits are usually well established, so they won't be easy to change, but change them you must if you want to enjoy the benefits of a healthy lifestyle. But what if you've tried and failed (miserably) to change your eating habits? If that's the case, it's time to ask for help from a higher authority.

God invites us to ask Him for the things we need, and He promises to hear our prayers as well as our thoughts. The Lord is always available and He's always ready to help us. And He knows precisely what we need. But He still instructs us to ask. So be fervent in prayer and don't hesitate to ask the Creator for the tools you need to accomplish His plan for your life. Then, get busy and expect the best. When you do your part, God will most certainly do His part. And great things are bound to happen.

More FROM GOD'S WORD

Until now you have asked for nothing in My name.
Ask and you will receive, that your joy may be complete.

JOHN 16:24 HCSB

The effective prayer of a righteous man can accomplish much.

JAMES 5:16 NASB

Your Father knows the things
you have need of before you ask Him.

MATTHEW 6:8 NKJV

You did not choose me, but I chose you and appointed
you to go and bear fruit—fruit that will last.
Then the Father will give you whatever you ask in my name.

JOHN 15:16 NIV

Do not be anxious about anything, but in everything, by prayer
and petition, with thanksgiving, present your requests to God.

PHILIPPIANS 4:6 NIV

ASKING GOD

It's important that you keep asking God to show you what He wants you to do. If you don't ask, you won't know.

STORMIE OMARTIAN

God will help us become the people we are meant to be, if only we will ask Him.

HANNAH WHITALL SMITH

We honor God by asking for great things when they are a part of His promise. We dishonor Him and cheat ourselves when we ask for molehills where He has promised mountains.

VANCE HAVNER

Are you serious about wanting God's guidance to become a personal reality in your life? The first step is to tell God that you know you can't manage your own life; that you need his help.

CATHERINE MARSHALL

God insists that we ask, not because He needs to know our situation, but because we need the spiritual discipline of asking.

CATHERINE MARSHALL

FOOD TIP

Keep Searching for Healthy Snacks

Take note of what healthy snacks your family actually enjoys.
If the grapes are a hit while the celery ends up in the garbage can,
focus on the fruit next time you go grocery shopping.

FITNESS TIP

If You Want More from Life, Ask More from God

If you're striving for better health—or if you're
pursuing any other worthy goal—ask God
(and keep asking Him) until He answers your prayers.

TODAY'S FOCUS

Think about the importance of asking
God for the things you really need.

32

ABOVE AND BEYOND THE TEMPTATIONS

Your adversary, the devil, prowls around like a roaring lion, seeking someone to devour.

1 PETER 5:8 NASB

Our world is teeming with distractions and temptations that can rob you of the physical, emotional, and spiritual fitness that might otherwise be yours. And if you're not careful, the stresses and struggles of everyday living can rob you of the peace that should rightfully be yours through Christ. So take time each day to have a personal training session with your Savior. Don't be satisfied with occasional visits to church on Sunday morning; build a relationship with Jesus that deepens day by day. When you do, you will most certainly encounter the subtle hand of the Father. Then, if you are wise, you will take His hand and follow God as He leads you on the path to a healthier, happier life.

Never before in the history of humankind have adults and children alike been offered access to so many spiritual snares. Never before has the Devil had so many tools. So beware. Take a stand against your enemy, and ask for God's protection. Because your adversary never takes a day off . . . and neither should you.

More FROM GOD'S WORD

No temptation has overtaken you but such as is common
to man; and God is faithful, who will not allow you
to be tempted beyond what you are able,
but with the temptation will provide the way of escape.

I CORINTHIANS 10:13 NASB

Put on the whole armor of God, that you may be able
to stand against the wiles of the devil.

EPHESIANS 6:11 NKJV

But encourage each other daily, while it is still called today,
so that none of you is hardened by sin's deception.

HEBREWS 3:13 HCSB

Let us lay aside every weight, and the sin
which so easily ensnares us, and let us run
with endurance the race that is set before us.

HEBREWS 12:1 NKJV

Do not be misled: "Bad company corrupts good character."

I CORINTHIANS 15:33 NIV

About Temptation

Temptations that have been anticipated, guarded against, and prayed about have little power to harm us. Jesus tells us to "keep watching and praying, that you may not come into temptation."

John MacArthur

It is easier to stay out of temptation than to get out of it.

Rick Warren

*It is not the temptations you have,
but the decision you make about them that counts.*

Billy Graham

*The first step on the way to victory
is to recognize the enemy.*

Corrie ten Boom

*Every temptation, directly or indirectly,
is the temptation to doubt and distrust God.*

John MacArthur

FOOD TIP

Take Control of Your Lunch

To eat healthy at the office, pack your own lunch instead
of eating out. Plan ahead, and be sure to pack a lunch
with healthy ingredients and reasonable portion sizes.

FITNESS TIP

Learn to Say No

In a world where high-calorie treats are plentiful and cheap,
it's wise to learn how to say no to your taste buds. When you
say no to unhealthy foods, you're saying yes to better health.

TODAY'S FOCUS

Think about the need to remain vigilant
in this temptation-filled world.

33

BE ENTHUSIASTIC

Whatever you do, do it enthusiastically,
as something done for the Lord and not for men.

COLOSSIANS 3:23 HCSB

If you're sincerely trying to improve your health and your diet, here's a hint: be enthusiastic about your plan and optimistic about the results. But don't stop there. As a Christian, you have many more reasons to be enthusiastic about your future. After all, your eternal destiny is secure. Christ died for your sins, and He wants you to experience life abundant and life eternal. And if you're beginning to reap the rewards of a new fitness regimen, you have yet another reason to celebrate. So what's not to get excited about?

Are you a passionate person and an enthusiastic Christian? Are you genuinely excited about your faith, your family, your fitness, and your future? Hopefully, you can answer these questions with a resounding yes. But if your passion for life has waned, it's time to slow down long enough to recharge your spiritual batteries and reorder your priorities.

Each new day is an opportunity to put God first and celebrate His creation. Today, take time to count your blessings and take stock of your opportunities. And while you're at it, ask God for strength. When you sincerely petition Him, He will give you everything you need to live enthusiastically and abundantly.

More FROM GOD'S WORD

Do your work with enthusiasm.
Work as if you were serving the Lord,
not as if you were serving only men and women.

EPHESIANS 6:7 NCV

But as for me, I will hope continually,
and will praise You yet more and more.

PSALM 71:14 NASB

Rejoice always! Pray constantly.
Give thanks in everything,
for this is God's will for you in Christ Jesus.

I THESSALONIANS 5:16–18 HCSB

Let the hearts of those who seek the LORD rejoice.
Look to the LORD and his strength; seek his face always.

I CHRONICLES 16:10–11 NIV

A happy heart makes the face cheerful,
but heartache crushes the spirit.

PROVERBS 15:13 NIV

ABOUT ENTHUSIASM

*Do the present duty—bear the present pain—
enjoy the present pleasure—and leave emotions
and "experiences" to look after themselves.*

C. S. LEWIS

*Those who have achieved excellence in the practice
of an art or profession have commonly been motivated
by great enthusiasm in their pursuit of it.*

JOHN KNOX

*Occupy your minds with good thoughts, or your enemy
will fill them with bad ones; unoccupied they cannot be.*

ST. THOMAS MORE

*Wherever you are, be all there. Live to the hilt
every situation you believe to be the will of God.*

JIM ELLIOT

*Do not let your happiness depend on something you may lose,
only upon the Beloved who will never pass away.*

C. S. LEWIS

FOOD TIP
Low Fat Isn't Always the Answer

Low fat doesn't mean low calories! Read the nutrition label.
Some foods may reduce fat but add more sugar to improve the taste.

FITNESS TIP
Too Much Screen Time?

Replace unnecessary screen time with
outdoor activities the whole family can enjoy.

TODAY'S FOCUS

Consider the possibility that an enthusiastic outlook
and a positive attitude can help you accomplish your goals.

34

BE CHEERFUL

A cheerful heart has a continual feast.

PROVERBS 15:15 HCSB

As Christians, we have so many reasons to be cheerful: God is in His heaven; He remains firmly in control; He loves us; and through His Son, He has offered us a path to eternal life. Despite these blessings, all of us will occasionally fall victim to the inevitable frustrations of everyday life. When we do, we should pause, take a deep breath, and remember how richly we've been blessed.

Cheerfulness is a gift that we give to others and to ourselves. The joy we give to others is reciprocal: whatever we give away is returned to us, oftentimes in greater measure. So make this promise to yourself and keep it: be a cheerful ambassador for Christ. He deserves no less, and neither, for that matter, do you.

More FROM GOD'S WORD

Rejoice always, pray without ceasing,
in everything give thanks; for this is the will
of God in Christ Jesus for you.

I THESSALONIANS 5:16–18 NKJV

Shout for joy to the LORD, all the earth. Worship the LORD
with gladness; come before him with joyful songs.

PSALM 100:1–2 NIV

Do everything without grumbling and arguing,
so that you may be blameless and pure.

PHILIPPIANS 2:14–15 HCSB

A cheerful heart is good medicine,
but a crushed spirit dries up the bones.

PROVERBS 17:22 NIV

This is the day that the LORD has made.
Let us rejoice and be glad today!

PSALM 118:24 NCV

About Cheerfulness

*It is possible to see God's will in every circumstance
and to accept it with singing instead of complaining.*

Lettie Cowman

*God is good, and heaven is forever.
And if those two facts don't cheer you up, nothing will.*

Marie T. Freeman

*The greatest honor you can give Almighty God is to live
gladly and joyfully because of the knowledge of His love.*

Juliana of Norwich

*The practical effect of Christianity is happiness,
therefore let it be spread abroad everywhere!*

C. H. Spurgeon

A life of intimacy with God is characterized by joy.

Oswald Chambers

FOOD TIP

Avoid Grocery Store Snack Attacks

Don't go grocery shopping when you're hungry!
Not only will you end up buying food you may not need,
but you're also more likely to splurge on unhealthy snacks.

FITNESS TIP

Pick the Right Fuel

If you place a high value on the body God has given you,
then place high importance on the foods you use to fuel it.
Fresh, natural, unprocessed foods are best.

TODAY'S FOCUS

Focus on the fact that a cheerful heart is a continual feast.

35

HEALTHY FRIENDSHIPS

As iron sharpens iron,
so people can improve each other.

PROVERBS 27:17 NCV

Our friends are gifts from above. God places them along our path and asks us to treat them with kindness, love, and respect. His Word teaches us that true friendship is both a blessing and a treasure.

Emily Dickinson spoke for friends of every generation when she observed, "My friends are my estate." Dickinson understood that friends are among our most treasured possessions. But unlike a stock certificate or a bank account, the value of true friendship is beyond measure.

Today, as you strive to improve your physical, spiritual, and emotional health, consider ways that you can encourage your friends to do likewise. When friends encourage friends, good things happen. And everybody wins.

More FROM GOD'S WORD

A friend loves at all times,
and a brother is born for adversity.

PROVERBS 17:17 NIV

It is good and pleasant when God's people
live together in peace!

PSALM 133:1 NCV

Dear friends, if God loved us in this way,
we also must love one another.

I JOHN 4:11 HCSB

Thine own friend, and thy father's friend, forsake not . . .

PROVERBS 27:10 KJV

Oil and incense bring joy to the heart,
and the sweetness of a friend is better than self-counsel.

PROVERBS 27:9 HCSB

ABOUT FRIENDS AND FRIENDSHIP

Friendship is one of the sweetest joys of life.
Many might have failed beneath the bitterness
of their trial had they not found a friend.

C. H. SPURGEON

In friendship, God opens your eyes to the glories of Himself.

JONI EARECKSON TADA

I cannot even imagine where I would be today were it not for
that handful of friends who have given me a heart full of joy.
Let's face it: friends make life a lot more fun.

CHARLES SWINDOLL

Our love to God is measured by our everyday fellowship
with others and the love it displays.

ANDREW MURRAY

A friend is one who makes me do my best.

OSWALD CHAMBERS

Food Tip

The Search for Soda Substitutes

Water with a hint of 100 percent juice
makes a flavorful substitute to sugary soda.

Fitness Tip

Find a Friend and Get Fit Together

Teamwork works. Friends help friends. When you have
a regular workout partner, you can motivate each other!

Today's Focus

Pray for your friends.

36

STAY POSITIVE

The LORD is my light and my salvation—
whom should I fear? The LORD is the stronghold of my life—
of whom should I be afraid?

PSALM 27:1 HCSB

Are you a glass-half-full optimist who expects God to do big things in your life? If so, you've increased the odds that you'll reach your goals. Whether you're striving to lose weight, or trying to improve your physical stamina, or attempting to achieve any other worthy goal, you're more likely to succeed if you believe you'll succeed.

If you're a thinking Christian, you have every reason to be confident about your future here on earth and your eternal future in heaven. After all, God has made quite a few promises to you, and He intends to keep every single one of them. But despite God's promises, and despite His love, you may, on occasion, find yourself caught up in the inevitable complications of everyday living. When you find yourself fretting about the inevitable ups and downs of daily life, it's time to slow yourself down, refocus your thoughts, and count your blessings.

Today, as you think about the goals you've set for yourself, trust your hopes, not your fears. And while you're at it, take time to celebrate God's blessings. His gifts are too numerous to calculate and too glorious to imagine. But it never hurts to try.

More FROM GOD'S WORD

Make me to hear joy and gladness . . .

PSALM 51:8 KJV

*"I say this because I know what I am planning for you,"
says the LORD. "I have good plans for you, not plans to hurt you.
I will give you hope and a good future."*

JEREMIAH 29:11 NCV

*This hope we have as an anchor of the soul,
a hope both sure and steadfast . . .*

HEBREWS 6:19 NASB

*Let us hold on to the confession of our hope without wavering,
for He who promised is faithful.*

HEBREWS 10:23 HCSB

*But if we look forward to something we don't have yet,
we must wait patiently and confidently.*

ROMANS 8:25 NLT

About The Power
of Positive Thoughts

Your life today is a result of your thinking yesterday.
Your life tomorrow will be determined by what you think today.

JOHN MAXWELL

No more imperfect thoughts. No more sad memories.
No more ignorance. My redeemed body will have
a redeemed mind. Grant me a foretaste of that perfect
mind as you mirror your thoughts in me today.

JONI EARECKSON TADA

All things work together for good. Fret not, nor fear!

LETTIE COWMAN

When you have vision, it affects your attitude.
Your attitude is optimistic rather than pessimistic.

CHARLES SWINDOLL

Positive thinking will let you do everything better
than negative thinking will.

ZIG ZIGLAR

Food Tip

Focus on the Positive

Trying to eat healthier foods? Don't focus on
all the foods you're not eating. Instead, focus on all
the fun new foods you are eating. Mangoes, anyone?

Fitness Tip

Positive Health Starts with a Positive Attitude

Fitness is a state of body, mind, and spirit.
Where your mind leads, your body will follow.

Today's Focus

Focus on ways that the self-fulfilling prophecy
can help you accomplish your goals.

37

THE GIFT OF
ENCOURAGEMENT

*But encourage each other daily, while it is still called today,
so that none of you is hardened by sin's deception.*

HEBREWS 3:13 HCSB

If you're trying to accomplish a worthy goal, it helps to have encouraging teammates. When other people believe in you, it's easier to believe in yourself. When other people cheer you on, it's easier to stay the course. When other people celebrate your progress, it's easier to keep making progress. So, as you continue on the path to improved health, be sure to invite a few encouraging friends along for the ride.

The world can be a difficult place, a place where we encounter the inevitable setbacks and slip-ups that are woven into the fabric of everyday life. So we all need boosters who are ready, willing, and able to cheer for us when the going gets tough.

Giving and receiving encouragement is the job of every Christian. And if you do the job well, you'll be a blessing to others, just as they will be a blessing to you.

More from God's Word

*Let us think about each other and help each other
to show love and do good deeds.*

Hebrews 10:24 ICB

*So encourage each other and give each other strength,
just as you are doing now.*

I Thessalonians 5:11 NCV

*When you talk, do not say harmful things,
but say what people need—words that will
help others become stronger. Then what you say
will do good to those who listen to you.*

Ephesians 4:29 NCV

*Now we exhort you, brethren, warn those who are unruly,
comfort the fainthearted, uphold the weak, be patient with all.*

I Thessalonians 5:14 NKJV

Bear one another's burdens, and so fulfill the law of Christ.

Galatians 6:2 NKJV

About Encouragement

Discouraged people don't need critics. They hurt enough already.
What they need is encouragement.
They need a refuge, a willing, caring, available someone.

Charles Swindoll

All around you are people whose lives are filled with trouble
and sorrow. They need your compassion and encouragement.

Billy Graham

Don't forget that a single sentence, spoken at the right moment,
can change somebody's whole perspective on life.
A little encouragement can go a long, long way.

Marie T. Freeman

When we are the comfort and encouragement to others, we are
sometimes surprised at how it comes back to us many times over.

Billy Graham

Doing something positive toward another person
is a practical approach to feeling good about yourself.

Barbara Johnson

FOOD TIP
The Clean-Plate Club Is for Kids

Don't be afraid to forfeit your membership in the Clean Plate Club! Contrary to the advice you may have received as a child, there's no universal law that says you must eat everything on your plate.

FITNESS TIP
Encouragement Helps, Teamwork Works

If you're trying to reshape your physique or your life, don't try to do it alone. Ask for the support and encouragement of your family members and friends. You'll improve your odds of success if you enlist your own cheering section.

TODAY'S FOCUS

Focus on being a source of encouragement to everyone you meet.

38

BE JOYFUL

This is the day which the LORD has made;
let us rejoice and be glad in it.

PSALM 118:24 NASB

The joy that the world offers is fleeting and incomplete: here today, gone tomorrow, not coming back anytime soon. But God's joy is different. His joy has staying power. In fact, it's a gift that never stops giving to those who welcome His Son into their hearts.

Psalm 100 reminds us to celebrate the lives that God has given us: "Shout for joy to the LORD, all the earth. Worship the LORD with gladness; come before Him with joyful songs" (v. 1–2 NIV). Yet sometimes, amid the inevitable complications and predicaments that are woven into the fabric of everyday life, we forget to rejoice. Instead of celebrating life, we complain about it. This is an understandable mistake, but a mistake nonetheless. As Christians, we are called by our Creator to live joyfully and abundantly. To do otherwise is to squander His spiritual gifts.

This day and every day, Christ offers you His peace and His joy. Accept it and share it with others, just as He has shared His joy with you.

More FROM GOD'S WORD

Rejoice in the Lord always. Again I will say, rejoice!

PHILIPPIANS 4:4 NKJV

I have spoken these things to you so that My joy
may be in you and your joy may be complete.

JOHN 15:11 HCSB

Until now you have asked for nothing in My name.
Ask and you will receive, that your joy may be complete.

JOHN 16:24 HCSB

So you also have sorrow now. But I will see you again.
Your hearts will rejoice, and no one will rob you of your joy.

JOHN 16:22 HCSB

Rejoice always, pray without ceasing, in everything give thanks;
for this is the will of God in Christ Jesus for you.

I THESSALONIANS 5:16–18 NKJV

ABOUT JOY

Joy is the great note all throughout the Bible.

OSWALD CHAMBERS

Joy is the serious business of heaven.

C. S. LEWIS

*Joy is the settled assurance that God is in control
of all the details of my life, the quiet confidence
that ultimately everything is going to be all right,
and the determined choice to praise God in all things.*

KAY WARREN

*It is possible to see God's will in every circumstance
and to accept it with singing instead of complaining.*

LETTIE COWMAN

Joy comes not from what we have but what we are.

C. H. SPURGEON

FOOD TIP
Slow Down!

Want to avoid overeating? Try eating more slowly. It takes about
twenty minutes for your stomach to send the message
to your brain that you're full. So, the more time you
take between bites, the fewer bites you'll eventually take.

FITNESS TIP
Get Outside and Play

Don't just get the kids off the video games—
get outside as a family. Everyone get exercise,
and it's also a great way to make family memories.

TODAY'S FOCUS

Think about the rewards of being a joyful Christian.

39

BE PATIENT

A man's wisdom gives him patience;
it is to his glory to overlook an offense.

PROVERBS 19:11 NIV

Most of us are impatient for God to grant us the desires of our heart. If we're trying to lose weight, we want to lose it immediately, if not sooner. And if we begin a new exercise regimen, we want to see results today, not tomorrow. But God may have other plans. He has created a world in which hard work is rewarded eventually, but not necessarily instantaneously. So, when God's timetable differs from our own, we must trust in His infinite wisdom and in His infinite love.

As busy men and women living in a fast-paced world, many of us find that waiting quietly for God is difficult. Yet He instructs us to be patient in all things. We must be patient with our families, with our friends, and even with ourselves. We must also be patient with our Creator as He unfolds His plan for our lives. And that's as it should be. After all, think how patient God has been with us.

More FROM GOD'S WORD

Patience of spirit is better than haughtiness of spirit.

ECCLESIASTES 7:8 NASB

But if we hope for what we do not yet have,
we wait for it patiently.

ROMANS 8:25 NIV

Be joyful in hope, patient in affliction,
faithful in prayer.

ROMANS 12:12 NIV

The LORD is good to those who depend on him,
to those who search for him. So it is good to wait
quietly for salvation from the LORD.

LAMENTATIONS 3:25–26 NLT

Better to be patient than powerful;
better to have self-control than to conquer a city.

PROVERBS 16:32 NLT

ABOUT PATIENCE

Patience is the companion of wisdom.

ST. AUGUSTINE

Bear with the faults of others
as you would have them bear with yours.

PHILLIPS BROOKS

Frustration is not the will of God.
There is time to do anything and everything
that God wants us to do.

ELISABETH ELLIOT

Today, take a complicated situation and with time,
patience, and a smile, turn it into
something positive—for you and for others.

JONI EARECKSON TADA

Patience graciously, compassionately, and with understanding,
judges the faults of others without unjust criticism.

BILLY GRAHAM

FOOD TIP

Not All Cereals Are Created Equal

Limit sugar at the breakfast table by choosing unsweetened cereal or cereal sweetened with fresh or dried fruits.

FITNESS TIP

Day In, Day Out

Your journey with God unfolds day by day, and that's precisely how your journey to an improved state of physical fitness must also unfold: moment by moment, day by day, year by year.

TODAY'S FOCUS

Think about ways that patience pays and impatience costs.

40

BE STRONG
AND DO YOUR DUTY

Be strong and courageous, and do the work.
Don't be afraid or discouraged, for the LORD God,
my God, is with you. He won't leave you or forsake you . . .

I CHRONICLES 28:20 HCSB

Staying fit and eating healthy foods requires diligence, determination, patience, and perseverance. So is it really worth all the trouble and pain? Absolutely. When you improve your health, you also improve your life.

But please don't think that your food-and-fitness efforts are for your benefit only. By increasing the chances that you'll live a longer, healthier, happier life, you're also performing an important duty for the people who love you and depend on you. And you're obeying the Creator who gave you life in the first place.

God wants you to take all your duties seriously, especially your duties to the people He's entrusted to your care: your family. By taking care of yourself, you're indirectly taking care of them too.

More FROM GOD'S WORD

*And we desire that each one of you show the same diligence
so as to realize the full assurance of hope until the end,
so that you will not be sluggish, but imitators of those
who through faith and patience inherit the promises.*

HEBREWS 6:11–12 NASB

So then each of us shall give account of himself to God.

ROMANS 14:12 NKJV

*I am He who searches the minds and hearts;
and I will give to each one of you according to your deeds.*

REVELATION 2:23 NASB

*Here is my final conclusion: Fear God and obey his commands,
for this is the duty of every person.*

ECCLESIASTES 12:13 NLT

*I must work the works of him that sent me,
while it is day: the night cometh, when no man can work.*

JOHN 9:4 KJV

About Duty

Our grand business is not to see what lies dimly at a distance,
but to do what lies closely at hand.

THOMAS CARLYLE

Don't bother to give God instructions; just report for duty.

CORRIE TEN BOOM

God never imposes a duty without giving time to do it.

JOHN RUSKIN

Discipleship usually brings us into the necessity
of choice between duty and desire.

ELISABETH ELLIOT

The present is the only time in which
any duty may be done or grace received.

C. S. LEWIS

FOOD TIP

Don't Skip Meals

Are you skipping meals? Don't do it. Skipping meals isn't healthy, and it isn't a sensible way to lose weight, either.

FITNESS TIP

Join in the Fun

Group exercise is a great way to stay fit and socialize at the same time. And as an additional benefit, your fellow fitness buffs will give you the encouragement you need to stick with your exercise plan.

TODAY'S FOCUS

Think about the rewards of a sensible
exercise regimen combined with a healthy diet.

41

DREAM BIG

Hope deferred makes the heart sick,
but a dream fulfilled is a tree of life.

PROVERBS 13:12 NLT

Do you consider the future to be friend or foe? Do you expect the best, and are you willing to work for it? If so, please consider the fact that the Lord does, indeed, help those who help themselves. And He's especially helpful to those who consult Him before they finalize their plans.

God's help is always available to those who ask. Our job, of course, is to seek His guidance and His strength as we seek to accomplish His plans for our lives.

If you're serious about achieving your fitness goals, remember to enlist God as your partner. Nothing is too difficult for Him, and no dreams are too big for Him—not even yours. When you do your part, He'll do His part, and great things are bound to happen. So live confidently, plan carefully, pray often, do your best, and leave the rest up to the Creator. You and He, working together, can move mountains. Lots of them.

More FROM GOD'S WORD

Hope deferred makes the heart sick.

PROVERBS 13:12 NKJV

*But we are hoping for something we do not have yet,
and we are waiting for it patiently.*

ROMANS 8:25 NCV

*Now may the God of hope fill you with all joy
and peace as you believe in Him so that you may overflow
with hope by the power of the Holy Spirit.*

ROMANS 15:13 HCSB

*Humble yourselves therefore under the mighty hand of God,
that he may exalt you in due time.*

I PETER 5:6 KJV

Where there is no vision, the people perish . . .

PROVERBS 29:18 KJV

ABOUT DREAMING BIG

Allow your dreams a place in your prayers and plans.
God-given dreams can help you move
into the future He is preparing for you.

BARBARA JOHNSON

Two types of voices command your attention today.
Negative ones fill your mind with doubt, bitterness,
and fear. Positive ones purvey hope and strength.
Which one will you choose to heed?

MAX LUCADO

God's gifts put man's best dreams to shame.

ELIZABETH BARRETT BROWNING

The presence of hope in the invincible
sovereignty of God drives out fear.

JOHN PIPER

When the dream of our heart is one that God has planted there,
a strange happiness flows into us. At that moment, the spiritual
resources of the universe are released to help us.

CATHERINE MARSHALL

FOOD TIP
The Less Processing, the Better

Generally speaking, you're better off sticking with fresh, unprocessed foods, not those highly processed factory-made foods.

FITNESS TIP
Don't Just Watch the Game, Get Out and Play It

Spending too much time watching sports on TV? Find a sport of your own—any form of exercise will do—and have just as much fun while improving your health.

TODAY'S FOCUS

Take a few minutes and jot down a few of your biggest dreams. Then, make it a habit to pray about your hopes and aspirations. When you talk to God about your dreams and seek His guidance, big things happen.

42

THE NEED FOR SELF-DISCIPLINE

Discipline yourself for the purpose of godliness.

I TIMOTHY 4:7 NASB

Time and again, God's Word makes it clear: He doesn't reward laziness, misbehavior, or apathy. To the contrary, He expects believers to discipline themselves. And that's precisely what He expects from you.

If you genuinely seek to be a faithful steward of your time, your talents, and your resources, you must adopt a disciplined approach to life. Otherwise, your talents may go unused and your resources may be squandered.

So, as you consider ways to enhance your health through proper diet and sensible exercise, remember this: life's greatest rewards are unlikely to fall into your lap; to the contrary, your greatest accomplishments will probably require lots of work and plenty of self-discipline. And that's perfectly okay with God, because He understands that self-discipline is actually a blessing, not a burden. Hopefully, you'll understand it too.

More FROM GOD'S WORD

Whatever you do, do your work heartily,
as for the Lord rather than for men.

COLOSSIANS 3:23 NASB

But the fruit of the Spirit is love, joy, peace,
patience, kindness, goodness, faith, gentleness, self-control.
Against such things there is no law.

GALATIANS 5:22–23 HCSB

Finishing is better than starting.
Patience is better than pride.

ECCLESIASTES 7:8 NLT

A final word: Be strong with the Lord's mighty power.

EPHESIANS 6:10 NLT

Better to be patient than powerful;
better to have self-control than to conquer a city.

PROVERBS 16:32 NLT

ABOUT SELF-DISCIPLINE

*To live out God's plan for your life calls for you
to discipline yourself and your body.
To push yourself. To deny yourself.*

ELIZABETH GEORGE

When love and skill work together, expect a masterpiece.

JOHN RUSKIN

*Pray as though everything depended on God.
Work as though everything depended on you.*

ST. AUGUSTINE

*The best preparation for the future is the present
well seen to, and the last duty done.*

GEORGE MACDONALD

*Decisions, demanded by work, become easier
and simpler where they are made not in the fear of men,
but only in the sight of God.*

DIETRICH BONHOEFFER

FOOD TIP

How Many Fruits and Vegetables?

How much is enough when it comes to fruits and vegetables? The general rule says they should fill half of your plate.

FITNESS TIP

It doesn't matter what you are trying to accomplish. It's all a matter of discipline.

WILMA RUDOLPH

TODAY'S FOCUS

Think about the rewards of self-discipline.

43

STAY HUMBLE

Therefore humble yourselves under the mighty
hand of God, that He may exalt you in due time,
casting all your care upon Him, for He cares for you.

1 PETER 5:6–7 NKJV

We humans are often tempted by a dangerous, debilitating sin: pride. Even though God's Word clearly warns us that pride is hazardous to our spiritual health, we're still tempted to brag about our accomplishments, and overstate them. We're tempted to puff ourselves up by embellishing our victories and concealing our defeats. But in truth, all of us are mere mortals who have many more reasons to be humble than prideful.

As Christians who have been saved, not by our own good works but by God's grace, how can we be prideful? The answer, of course, is that if we are honest with ourselves and with our God, we simply can't be boastful. We must, instead, be filled with humble appreciation for the things God has done. Our good works are miniscule compared to His. Whatever happens, the Lord deserves the credit, not us. And if we're wise, we'll give Him all the credit He deserves.

More FROM GOD'S WORD

Always be humble, gentle, and patient,
accepting each other in love.

EPHESIANS 4:2 NCV

For everyone who exalts himself will be humbled,
and the one who humbles himself will be exalted.

LUKE 14:11 HCSB

Therefore, God's chosen ones, holy and loved,
put on heartfelt compassion, kindness,
humility, gentleness, and patience.

COLOSSIANS 3:12 HCSB

Blessed are the meek: for they shall inherit the earth.

MATTHEW 5:5 KJV

Humble yourselves in the sight of the Lord,
and he shall lift you up.

JAMES 4:10 KJV

About Humility

Pride builds walls between people,
humility builds bridges.

RICK WARREN

Humility is not thinking less of yourself,
it's thinking of yourself less.

RICK WARREN

The holy man is the most humble man you can meet.

OSWALD CHAMBERS

God measures people by the small dimensions
of humility and not by the bigness of their achievements
or the size of their capabilities.

BILLY GRAHAM

Faith itself cannot be strong where humility is weak.

C. H. SPURGEON

FOOD TIP

Two for the Price of One

When eating out, consider splitting up the main
dish with family or friends. Not only do you
control portion size, but you also save money.

FITNESS TIP

Recharge Your Batteries with Exercise

At a loss for energy? Try exercise instead of caffeine.
It may sound counterintuitive, but exercise just
might be all that you need to face the day ahead.

TODAY'S FOCUS

Think about God's commandment to be humble.
Why does the Lord instruct us to be humble,
and what blessings will be ours when we obey Him?

44

No Complaints

Be hospitable to one another without complaining.

I Peter 4:9 HCSB

Most of us have more blessings than we can count, yet we still find things to complain about. To complain, of course, is not only shortsighted, but it is also a serious roadblock on the path to spiritual abundance. But in our weakest moments we still grumble, whine, and moan. Sometimes we give voice to our complaints, and on other occasions, we manage to keep our protestations to ourselves. But even when no one else hears our complaints, God does.

Would you like to feel more comfortable about your circumstances and your life? Then promise yourself that you'll do whatever it takes to ensure that you focus your thoughts and energy on the major blessings you've received, not the minor hardships you must occasionally endure.

So the next time you're tempted to complain about the inevitable frustrations of everyday living, don't do it. Today and every day, make it a practice to count your blessings, not your inconveniences. It's the truly decent way to live.

More FROM GOD'S WORD

Do everything without complaining or arguing.
Then you will be innocent and without any wrong.

PHILIPPIANS 2:14–15 NCV

A fool's displeasure is known at once,
but whoever ignores an insult is sensible.

PROVERBS 12:16 HCSB

Those who consider themselves religious
and yet do not keep a tight rein on their tongues
deceives themselves, and their religion is worthless.

JAMES 1:26 NIV

My dear brothers and sisters, always be willing
to listen and slow to speak.

JAMES 1:19 NCV

Those who guard their lips preserve their lives,
but those who speak rashly will come to ruin.

PROVERBS 13:3 NIV

About Complaining

*Thanksgiving or complaining—these words express
two contrasting attitudes of the souls of God's children.
The soul that gives thanks can find comfort in everything;
the soul that complains can find comfort in nothing.*

HANNAH WHITALL SMITH

*If we have our eyes upon ourselves, our problems,
and our pain, we cannot lift our eyes upward.*

BILLY GRAHAM

*Grumbling and gratitude are, for the child of God,
in conflict. Be grateful and you won't grumble.
Grumble and you won't be grateful.*

BILLY GRAHAM

*Don't complain. The more you complain about things,
the more things you'll have to complain about.*

E. STANLEY JONES

*It is always possible to be thankful for what is given
rather than to complain about what is not given.
One or the other becomes a habit of life.*

ELISABETH ELLIOT

FOOD TIP

Sometimes Water Works

Hungry for a snack? Try drinking water.
It's common to mistake thirst for hunger.

FITNESS TIP

It's Up to You

Never blame other people for the current state
of your health. It's your body; it's your responsibility.

TODAY'S FOCUS

Try to keep track of the times you complain,
either to someone else or to yourself. Also,
make note of the times you express gratitude to the Lord.
Do you spend more time complaining or praising?

45

Trust Him

*Trust in the LORD with all your heart,
and lean not on your own understanding;
in all your ways acknowledge Him,
and He shall direct your paths.*

PROVERBS 3:5–6 NKJV

If we genuinely desire to lead heathier, happier lives, we need wisdom. And if we're willing to search for real wisdom, we can always find it in a book like no other: the Holy Bible. The search for wisdom should be a lifelong journey, not a destination. We should continue to read, to watch, and to learn new things as long as we live. But it's not enough to learn new things or to memorize the great biblical truths; we must also live by them.

So what will you learn today? Will you take time to feed your mind and fill your heart? Will you trust God and the guidebook He has given you? Hopefully so, because the Lord's plans and His promises are waiting for you there, inside the covers of the book He wrote. It contains the essential wisdom you'll need to navigate the seas of life and land safely on that distant shore.

More FROM GOD'S WORD

In quietness and trust is your strength . . .

ISAIAH 30:15 NASB

The fear of man is a snare, but the one
who trusts in the LORD is protected.

PROVERBS 29:25 HCSB

Those who trust in the LORD are like Mount Zion.
It cannot be shaken; it remains forever.

PSALM 125:1 HCSB

Jesus said, "Don't let your hearts be troubled.
Trust in God, and trust in me."

JOHN 14:1 NCV

The LORD is my rock, my fortress,
and my deliverer, my God,
my mountain where I seek refuge.
My shield, the horn of my salvation, my stronghold,
my refuge, and my Savior.

II SAMUEL 22:2–3 HCSB

ABOUT TRUSTING GOD

One of the marks of spiritual maturity
is the quiet confidence that God is in control,
without the need to understand why He does what He does.

CHARLES SWINDOLL

Never yield to gloomy anticipation.
Place your hope and confidence in God.
He has no record of failure.

LETTIE COWMAN

Never be afraid to trust an unknown future to a known God.

CORRIE TEN BOOM

When a train goes through a tunnel and it gets dark,
you don't throw away your ticket and jump off.
You sit still and trust the engineer.

CORRIE TEN BOOM

Faith and obedience are bound up in the same bundle.
He that obeys God, trusts God; and he that trusts God, obeys God.

C. H. SPURGEON

FOOD TIP

Don't Make Screen Time Snack Time

Avoid snacking in front of the TV or the computer. It's far too easy to mindlessly overeat when you're focusing on something else.

FITNESS TIP

Keep Moving around the House

Spring-cleaning is exercise too! Keep your family active by vacuuming, washing the car, and doing yard work together.

TODAY'S FOCUS

Remember some of the ways God has protected you in the past. Let these experiences serve as definitive proof that you can trust Him now and forever.

46

Beware the Addictions

Be sober! Be on the alert! Your adversary the Devil is prowling around like a roaring lion, looking for anyone he can devour.

I Peter 5:8 HCSB

Avoiding addictions is an integral part of staying fit. The dictionary defines *addiction* as "the compulsive need for a habit-forming substance; the condition of being habitually and compulsively occupied with something." That definition is accurate, but incomplete. For Christians, addiction has an additional meaning: it means compulsively worshiping something other than God.

Ours is a society that often glamorizes the use of drugs, alcohol, cigarettes, and other addictive substances. So unless you're living on a deserted island, you know people who are full-blown addicts—probably lots of people. If you, or someone you love, is suffering from the blight of addiction, remember this: help is available. Many people have experienced addiction and lived to tell about it, so never abandon hope. With God, all things are possible.

And if you're one of those fortunate people who hasn't started experimenting with addictive substances, congratulations! You have just spared yourself a lifetime of headaches and heartaches.

More FROM GOD'S WORD

Thou shalt have no other gods before me.

EXODUS 20:3 KJV

*Do not carouse with drunkards and gluttons,
for they are on their way to poverty.*

PROVERBS 23:20–21 NLT

*Let us walk properly, as in the day,
not in revelry and drunkenness,
not in lewdness and lust, not in strife and envy.*

ROMANS 13:13 NKJV

*But the Lord is faithful; he will make you strong
and guard you from the evil one.*

II THESSALONIANS 3:3 NLT

*Do not be drunk with wine, which will ruin you,
but be filled with the Spirit.*

EPHESIANS 5:18 NCV

About Addiction

*People who have never had an addiction
don't understand how hard it can be.*

PAYNE STEWART

Rule your desires lest your desires rule you.

PUBLILIUS SYRUS

*'Tis easier to suppress the first desire
than to satisfy all that follow it.*

BEN FRANKLIN

*The chains of habit are too weak to be felt
until they are too strong to be broken.*

SAMUEL JOHNSON

*Ill habits gather by unseen degrees.
As brooks make rivers, and rivers run to seas.*

JOHN DRYDEN

FOOD TIP
Don't Worship Thinness

Don't equate thinness with happiness. You need not be rail-thin
to be happy, healthy, and well adjusted. And don't be obsessive
about your diet; your life shouldn't revolve around food.

FITNESS TIP
It's a Very Wise Choice

One of the wisest choices you can make is to take care of your
body. That means saying yes to a healthy lifestyle and no
to any substance that has the potential to harm you.

TODAY'S FOCUS

Spend a few moments considering the terrible costs that addictions
impose on individuals and society as a whole. And as you
contemplate the pain of addiction, remember that help
is always available and that God can move mountains.

47

REAL WORSHIP

I was glad when they said unto me,
Let us go into the house of the LORD.

PSALM 122:1 KJV

What does worship have to do with fitness? That depends on how you define worship. If you consider worship to be a Sunday-only activity that occurs inside the four walls of your local church, then fitness and worship may seem totally unrelated. But if you view worship as an activity that impacts every facet of your life—if you consider worship to be something far more than a one-day-a-week obligation—then you understand that every aspect of your life is a form of worship. And that includes keeping your body physically fit.

Whenever we become distracted by worldly pursuits that put God in second place, we inevitably pay the price of our misplaced priorities. A better strategy, of course, is to worship Him every day of the week, beginning with a regular early-morning devotional.

Every day provides opportunities to put God where He belongs: at the center of our lives. When we do so, we worship not just with our words, but also with our deeds. And one way that we can honor our Heavenly Father is by treating our bodies with care and respect.

More FROM GOD'S WORD

Happy are those who hear the joyful call to worship,
for they will walk in the light of your presence, LORD.

PSALM 89:15 NLT

God is Spirit, and those who worship Him
must worship in spirit and truth.

JOHN 4:24 HCSB

For where two or three are gathered together
in My name, I am there among them.

MATTHEW 18:20 HCSB

Worship the LORD with gladness. Come before him,
singing with joy. Acknowledge that the LORD is God! He made us,
and we are his. We are his people, the sheep of his pasture.

PSALM 100:2–3 NLT

All the earth will worship You and sing praise to You.
They will sing praise to Your name.

PSALM 66:4 HCSB

About Worship

Worship is an inward reverence,
the bowing down of the soul in the presence of God.

Elizabeth George

Learn to shut out the distractions
that keep you from truly worshiping God.

Billy Graham

We must worship in truth.
Worship is not just an emotional exercise
but a response of the heart built on truth about God.

Erwin Lutzer

Worship is focus.

Beth Moore

Worship in the truest sense takes place
only when our full attention is on God—
His glory, majesty, love, and compassion.

Billy Graham

FOOD TIP

The Search for Calcium

Calcium doesn't only come from a glass of milk! For more variety,
try other calcium-rich foods like low-fat, unsweetened yogurt.

FITNESS TIP

It is almost impossible to walk rapidly and be unhappy.

DR. HOWARD MURPHY

TODAY'S FOCUS

Think about what worship means to you.
And make note of at least one step that you
can take to enhance your worship experience.

48

GOD'S PROMISES NEVER FAIL

*Let us hold on to the confession of our hope without wavering,
for He who promised is faithful.*

HEBREWS 10:23 HCSB

The Bible contains promises upon which you, as a believer, can depend. When the Creator of the universe makes a pledge to you, He will keep it. No exceptions.

You can think of the Bible as a written contract between you and your Heavenly Father. When you fulfill your obligations to Him, the Lord will most certainly fulfill His covenant to you.

When we accept Christ into our hearts, God promises us the opportunity to experience contentment, peace, and spiritual abundance. But more importantly, God promises that the priceless gift of eternal life will be ours. These promises should give us comfort. With God on our side, we have absolutely nothing to fear in this world and everything to hope for in the next.

More FROM GOD'S WORD

Sustain me as You promised, and I will live;
do not let me be ashamed of my hope.

PSALM 119:116 HCSB

They will bind themselves to the LORD
with an eternal covenant that will never be forgotten.

JEREMIAH 50:5 NLT

My God is my rock, in whom I take refuge,
my shield and the horn of my salvation . . .

II SAMUEL 22:2–3 NIV

He heeded their prayer, because they put their trust in him.

I CHRONICLES 5:20 NKJV

As for God, his way is perfect: the word of the LORD is tried:
he is a buckler to all those that trust in him.

PSALM 18:30 KJV

About God's Promises

Gather the riches of God's promises. Nobody can take away from you those texts from the Bible which you have learned by heart.

CORRIE TEN BOOM

Don't let obstacles along the road to eternity shake your confidence in God's promises.

DAVID JEREMIAH

Beloved, God's promises can never fail to be accomplished, and those who patiently wait can never be disappointed, for a believing faith leads to realization.

LETTIE COWMAN

The Bible is God's book of promises, and unlike the books of man, it does not change or go out of date.

BILLY GRAHAM

Let God's promises shine on your problems.

CORRIE TEN BOOM

Food Tip

The Power of Protein

Protein is key to building and repairing muscles! Meat doesn't have the monopoly, either. Soy products, unsalted nuts, beans, and peas are also good sources of protein.

Fitness Tip

God's Commandments Apply to Your Physical Health Too

If you tend to divide your life into two categories, "spiritual" and "other," it's time to reconsider. God intends you to apply His commandments to every aspect of your life, and that includes your physical and emotional health too.

Today's Focus

Think about the promises God has made to you. And rejoice!

49

God First, Everything Else Second

You shall have no other gods before Me.

EXODUS 20:3 NKJV

For most of us, these are very busy times. We have obligations at home, at work, at school, or on social media. In between these duties, we try to carve out time for exercise and recreation. From the moment we rise until we drift off to sleep at night, we have things to do and people to contact. So how do we find time for God? We must make time for Him, plain and simple. When we put God first, we're blessed. But when we succumb to the pressures and temptations of the world, we inevitably pay a price for our misguided priorities.

In the book of Exodus, God warns that we should put no gods before Him. Yet all too often, we place our Lord in second, third, or fourth place as we focus on other things. When we place anything above our love for God—even a noble goal such as improved physical health—we forfeit a certain measure of peace that might otherwise be ours.

In the wilderness, Satan offered Jesus earthly power and unimaginable riches, but Jesus refused. Instead, He chose to worship His Heavenly Father. We must do likewise by putting God first and worshiping Him only. God must come first. Always first.

195

More FROM GOD'S WORD

Therefore, whether you eat or drink,
or whatever you do, do all to the glory of God.

I CORINTHIANS 10:31 NKJV

How happy is everyone who fears the LORD,
who walks in His ways!

PSALM 128:1 HCSB

But prove yourselves doers of the word,
and not merely hearers who delude themselves.

JAMES 1:22 NASB

We love him, because he first loved us.

I JOHN 4:19 KJV

For this is the love of God, that we keep His commandments.
And His commandments are not burdensome.

I JOHN 5:3 NKJV

PUTTING GOD FIRST

*The most important thing you must decide
to do every day is put the Lord first.*

ELIZABETH GEORGE

*Jesus Christ is the first and last, author and finisher, beginning
and end, alpha and omega, and by Him all other things hold
together. He must be first or nothing. God never comes next!*

VANCE HAVNER

Christ is either Lord of all, or He is not Lord at all.

HUDSON TAYLOR

*God wants to be in our leisure time as much
as He is in our churches and in our work.*

BETH MOORE

*Even the most routine part of your day
can be a spiritual act of worship.*

SARAH YOUNG

FOOD TIP

Cut Out Candy

Candy provides a few moments of taste-bud delight, but when
the candy's gone, so is the delight. But the calories remain.
So when selecting a snack, choose fresh fruit instead of candy.

FITNESS TIP

Take to the Streets

The more you walk, the healthier you'll be.
So when you have the time, walk, don't drive.

TODAY'S FOCUS

Think about the need to put God first in your life.
And think about the cost of not putting Him first.

50

SHARE THE GOOD NEWS

For God has not given us a spirit of fear and timidity,
but of power, love, and self-discipline. So you must never
be ashamed to tell others about our Lord.

II TIMOTHY 1:7–8 NLT

We live in a world that desperately needs the healing message of Jesus Christ. And every believer, each in his or her own way, bears a personal responsibility for sharing that message.

In his second letter to Timothy, Paul offers a message to believers of every generation when he writes, "God has not given us a spirit of timidity" (1:7 NASB). Paul's meaning is clear: When sharing our testimonies, we, as Christians, must be courageous, forthright, and unashamed.

If you've been transformed by God's only begotten Son, you know how He has touched your heart and changed your life. Now it's your turn to share the good news with others. And remember: now is the perfect time to share your testimony, because later may quite simply be too late.

More FROM GOD'S WORD

*And I say to you, anyone who acknowledges
Me before men, the Son of Man will also
acknowledge him before the angels of God.*

LUKE 12:8 HCSB

*All those who stand before others and say they believe in me,
I will say before my Father in heaven that they belong to me.*

MATTHEW 10:32 NCV

*When they had prayed, the place where they were assembled
was shaken, and they were all filled with the Holy Spirit
nd began to speak God's message with boldness.*

ACTS 4:31 HCSB

*Then He said to them, "Go into all the world
and preach the gospel to the whole creation."*

MARK 16:15 HCSB

*You must worship Christ as Lord of your life. And if you are
asked about your Christian hope, always be ready to explain it.*

I PETER 3:15 NLT

ABOUT YOUR TESTIMONY

What is your story? Be ready to share it
when the Lord gives you the opportunity.

BILLY GRAHAM

How many people have you made homesick for God?

OSWALD CHAMBERS

The enemy's hope for Christians is that we will either be so
ineffective we have no testimony, or we'll ruin the one we have.

BETH MOORE

When your heart is ablaze with the love of God, then you love
other people—especially the rip-snorting sinners—so much that
you dare to tell them about Jesus with no apologies and no fear.

CATHERINE MARSHALL

Heads are won by reasoning,
but hearts are won by witness-bearing.

C. H. SPURGEON

FOOD TIP

Be Food-Smart

Educate yourself on which foods are healthy
and which foods aren't. Take time to read labels,
and learn the basics of proper nutrition. Then, use
common sense and discipline in planning your diet.

FITNESS TIP

A Healthy Lifestyle Is Part of His Plan

Since God loves you, and since He wants the
very best for you, don't you believe that He also wants
you to enjoy a healthy lifestyle? Of course He does.
And since He wants it, shouldn't you want it too?

TODAY'S FOCUS

Consider the eternal implications of sharing your testimony.
Then, think of people who need to hear about Jesus from you.